GENERAL quizzes
KNOWLEDGE

ART · PLACES · MUSIC · BOOKS

THE QUIZ BOOK COMPANY

First published in 2004 by
The Quiz Book Company Ltd
Bardfield Centre,
Great Bardfield, Essex, CM7 4SL

ISBN 1-84236-503-7

Printed in India

Some of the material in this book has been used previously
in The Great Big Quiz Book and Sensational Quiz Books.
Other questions written by Chris Rigby.

QUIZ 1

• •

1   Who was the first author to have his novels serialised?

2   Who wrote Kane and Abel?

3   Who was Hans Christian Andersen?

4   What famous character did Richmal Crompton create?

5   Who has written well over 500 romantic novels?

6   Who was Robert Browning?

7   What is the Melody Maker?

8   Who was Geoffrey Chaucer?

9   What was the surname of the family of writers whose first names were Osbert, Sacheverell and Edith?

10 Who was the author of the Noddy books?

ANSWERS

1. Charles Dickens. 2. Jeffrey Archer. 3. Danish author of fairy stories.
4. William Brown - Just William. 5. Barbara Cartland. 6. Poet, and husband of Elizabeth Barrett Browning. 7. A weekly newspaper dealing with pop, rock and dance music. 8. English poet and author of The Canterbury Tales.
9. Sitwell. 10. Enid Blyton.

QUIZ 2

• •

1 What is 'mulligatawny'?

2 A 20th wedding anniversary is associated with gifts made of which material?

3 What is a 'filibuster'? Is it (a) a set of delaying tactics, (b) padding on upholstery or (c) a medieval weapon?

4 Why are 'red-letter days' so called?

5 What is the zip code for the US state of Maine?

6 What is the largest desert in the world?

7 What is a group of beavers called?

8 What is the last letter in the Greek alphabet?

9 During which months does Ramadan, the Muslim period of fasting, take place?

10 What does the international car index mark 'E' stand for?

ANSWERS

1. A kind of soup (a thick curry-flavoured meat soup). 2. China. 3. (a) A set of delaying tactics. 4. From the red letters used in church calendars to show saints' days and feasts. 5. ME. 6. The Sahara Desert. 7. Colony. 8. Omega. 9. May and June. 10. Spain.

QUIZ 3

• •

1   In which city is the famous 'Western Wall', or 'Wailing Wall'?

2   With what did Snow White's stepmother tempt her?

3   In the desert, what two things did the Israelites eat?

4   What substance forms the padding around the eyeball?

5   Who, in his speech in the House of Commons on 4 April 1940, said 'Hitler has missed the bus'?

6   Who is the French clothes designer born in 1936 particularly known for his efforts to bring fashionable clothes to ordinary people on a large scale?

7   What, in music, is a composition written as a setting of the Mass for the dead?

8   In which church are English monarchs usually crowned?

9   In which Oscar Wilde play is 'Jack' found in a handbag?

10   What do the words 'status quo' mean?

ANSWERS

1. Jerusalem. 2. A poisoned apple. 3. Manna and quail. 4. Fat. 5. Neville Chamberlain. 6. Yves Saint Laurent. 7. Requiem. 8. Westminster Abbey. 9. The Importance of Being Earnest.

QUIZ 4

1 What is the English term for the drink known in Scotland as 'Heavy'?

2 What kind of apes live on the Rock of Gibraltar?

3 What is the chief respiratory muscle called?

4 Which Scottish essayist is quoted as saying, 'History is the essence of innumerable biographies.'?

5 Which woman is holding up a torch in her right hand and represents freedom?

6 By what is SIDS more commonly known?

7 Who exclaimed 'Eureka' ('I've found it!') when noticing that his body displaced the water in his bath?

8 What is the name of a serpent, lizard or dragon reputed to kill by its breath or look?

9 What is the English title for the book of the Bible composed of 'sacred songs sung to Musical Accompaniment'?

10 Upon which instrument, played before or during a Church service, is a 'voluntary' played?

ANSWERS

1. Bitter. 2. Barbary Apes. 3. Diaphragm. 4. Thomas Carlyle. 5. Statue of Liberty. 6. Cot Death (Sudden Infant Death Syndrome). 7. Archimedes – Greek mathematician and scientist. 8. Basilisk. 9. Psalms. 10. Organ.

QUIZ 5

• •

1   In Shakespeare's *Julius Caesar*, with which famous words did 'Julius Caesar' receive his wounds from 'Brutus'?

2   What is the sweetener used to make Greek baklava?

3   What kind of farming is arable farming?

4   Who was the first leader of the Soviet Union, from 1918–24?

5   On crossing the Rubicon in 49bc, which Roman general said: 'The die is cast'?

6   What dish is made up of the following ingredients; sheep's offal, suet, oats and spices?

7   In what part of the body are the bones, the tibia and fibula?

8   What does DAT stand for?

9   How did a 'cockatrice', the creature of classical mythology hatched from a cock's egg, supposedly kill?

10 'The Lord is my Shepherd, I shall not want'. Of which Psalm is this the first line?

ANSWERS

1. 'Et tu, Brute?'. 2. Honey. 3. Crops. 4. Vladimir Ilyich Lenin. 5. Julius Caesar. 6. Haggis. 7. Leg (calf). 8. Digital Audio Tape. 9. By means of a death-dealing glance. 10. 23.

QUIZ 6

1 What name do we give to a native or inhabitant of Manchester?

2 For which US state is KY the abbreviation?

3 In his poem *The Pied Piper of Hamelin*, who wrote: 'They fought the dogs and killed the cats, And bit the babies in the cradles'?

4 What is the Italian name for the pudding translated as 'Pick-me-up'?

5 What is the sour ingredient added to a 'Whiskey Sour'?

6 Which animal is associated with 'Paddy McGinty'?

7 How much does a magnum hold?

8 Who wrote The Portrait of a Lady?

9 What does 'ad hoc' mean?

10 To which sport does the 'butterfly' stroke belong?

ANSWERS

1. Mancunian. 2. Kentucky. 3. Robert Browning. 4. 'Tiramisu'. 5. Lemon. 6. Goat. 7. One and a half litres or 2 normal bottles. 8. Henry James. 9. For a specific purpose. 10. Swimming.

QUIZ 7

1 How many lines does a limerick always have?

2 In one of his songs, who wrote 'Absence makes the heart grow fonder, Isle of Beauty, Fare thee well!'?

3 What do the initials of J. F. stand for in J. F. Kennedy, US president from 1961–63?

4 The cygnet is the young of which creature?

5 Pancreatic juice is strongly acidic. True or false?

6 In music, for what time of day is the performance of an 'aubade' originally intended?

7 What is the title of the novel by John Steinbeck about two itinerant farm labourers, one of huge strength and weak mind, exploited and protected by the other?

8 'In the beginning God created the heaven and the earth'. From which book of the Bible is this quoted?

9 Who rode the mythological 'hippocampus' – a sea horse, with a horse's forelegs and the tail of a fish or dolphin?

10 How many players are there in a hockey team?

ANSWERS

1. Five. 2. Thomas Haynes Bayly. 3. John Fitzgerald. 4. Swan. 5. False. It is strongly alkaline. 6. Morning. 7. *Of Mice and Men*. 8. Genesis. 9. Neptune. 10. 11.

QUIZ 8

. . . .

1 What do we call a young frog?

2 When dried, what do we call plums?

3 What does the Latin term 'in extremis' mean?

4 From which country does acupuncture originate?

5 What do griffins, creatures of classical mythology, look like?

6 Who was the tyrannical prime minister of Kampuchea from 1975–79?

7 In music, when a concerto is played, what else, apart from the orchestra, is required?

8 What is the traditional name for the Wednesday on which Lent begins?

9 What term do we give to the hours when pubs are open for the sale of alcoholic drinks?

10 Who played 'James Bond' in the film, *Moonraker*?

ANSWERS

1. Tadpole. 2. Prunes. 3. At the point of death, in extremity. 4. China. 5. They have an eagle's head and wings, and a lion's body and tail. 6. Pol Pot. 7. A solo instrument. 8. Ash Wednesday. 9. Licensing hours. 10. Roger Moore.

QUIZ 9

1 On which main river is Bristol situated?

2 Java, Columbian and Kenyan are types of what?

3 Named after a famous British statesman, what do we call a rubber boot without fastenings that reaches the knee?

4 Which smoked fish is called a kipper?

5 To which Roman general are the words 'Veni, vidi, vici', 'I came, I saw, I conquered', attributed?

6 In musical terms, a 'humoresque' is a playful or humorous composition. True or false?

7 In which English town is the traditional Goose Fair held, taking place on the first Thursday, Friday and Saturday in October?

8 Who wrote *Three Men In a Boat*?

9 What does 'per annum' mean?

10 When we want something 'quid pro quo', do we want something for nothing?

ANSWERS

1. Avon. 2. Coffee. 3. Wellington boot. 4. Herring. 5. Julius Caesar. 6. True. 7. Nottingham. 8. Jerome K. Jerome. 9. Annually. 10. No, we want something for something, an equal value exchange.

QUIZ 10

1 What is the traditional name of the dish made of sausages in batter?

2 What type of fish are plaice, sole and halibut?

3 Which capital city stands on the River Liffey?

4 Which Greek philosopher is quoted as saying, 'What we have to learn to do, we learn by doing'?

5 Founded in 1934, what is the name of the public school which became co-educational in 1972, near the coast in north-east Scotland?

6 On what day does Lent finish?

7 Who played the young 'John Connor' in the film *Terminator 2*?

8 In golf, what is an 'eagle'?

9 What are the three green coloured properties in the game of 'Monopoly'?

10 With which disease is the drug L-dopa originally associated?

ANSWERS

1. 'Toad in the Hole'. 2. Flat fish, salt water fish. 3. Dublin. 4. Aristotle. 5. Gordonstoun. 6. The day before Easter. 7. Edward Furlong. 8. Score of two strokes under par for the hole. 9. Bond Street, Regent Street and Oxford Street. 10. Parkinson's disease.

QUIZ 11

. . . .

1   Which fruit was traditionally eaten on Mothering and Palm Sundays?

2   What is a cliché?

3   On which foodstuff does the enzyme amylase found in the pancreas specifically act?

4   Who do we call the young of a deer?

5   From which book does the quotation 'Open Sesame!' come?

6   From which country comes the paso doble?

7   What is the name of the last book of the Bible?

8   What is the name of the racecourse near Chichester in West Sussex?

9   Who walks in a dream through the looking-glass in a book by Lewis Carroll?

10 What is the target number in the card game 'Pontoon'?

ANSWERS

1. Figs. 2. A phrase that has become worn out and emptied of meaning by over-frequent and careless use. 3. Starch. 4. Fawn. 5. *The History of Ali Baba*. 6. Spain. 7. Revelation. 8. Goodwood. 9. 'Alice'. 10. 21.

QUIZ 12

• •

1 What is the alternative name for the 'Pareto principle'?

2 What is 'lb' the abbreviation for?

3 In Cockney rhyming slang, what does 'frog and toad' refer to?

4 What is a samovar? Is it (a) a system of secret printing, (b) a metal urn for making tea or (c) a kind of sweater?

5 What is the former name of Myanmar?

6 What do electroencephalographs record?

7 In which book of the Bible is the hippopotamus-like beast, the behemoth, described?

8 In which town can you see the 'Bayeux Tapestry'?

9 What are 'hash browns'?

10 In music, what sort of scene is a 'pastorale' suggesting?

ANSWERS

1. The 80/20 rule. 2. Pounds (weight). 3. Road. 4. (b) A metal urn for making tea. 5. Burma. 6. Electrical activity in the brain. 7. Job. 8. Bayeux. 9. Fried onion and potato cakes. 10. Rural scene.

QUIZ 13

• •

1 Cations have a net positive charge and anions a net negative charge. True or false?

2 What is the chief element used in hydrotherapy?

3 Into what two types of events is athletics divided?

4 What is the name of the stiff, felt hat with a rounded crown and narrow brim?

5 What is the name of the youth in Greek mythology who was renowned for his great beauty?

6 What do electrocardiographs record?

7 What, in gardening, is bolting?

8 From whom do these words originally come: 'Don't count your chickens before they are hatched'?

9 What kind of 'ship' is a 'zeppelin'?

10 In the film Schindler's List, what was the colour of the little girl's coat shown in colour in the black and white scenes?

ANSWERS

1. True. 2. Water. 3. Track events and field events. 4. Bowler. 5. Adonis. 6. Heartbeats. 7. Premature running to seed. 8. Aesop, in his fable The Milkmaid and her Pail. 9. Airship. 10. Red.

QUIZ 14

. . . .

1 To what kind of person does the expression 'Walter Mitty' refer?

2 In which novel by George Orwell did 'Napolean' feature?

3 In 'Scrabble' what does the letter 'Z' score?

4 What is the name for a man's hat with a round, flat crown and a brim that can be turned down as well as up?

5 In which film did Henry Fonda play alongside his daughter as her father?

6 What does IVF stand for?

7 What is the capital of Austria?

8 What is the name used to describe pig-offal loaf?

9 What is the name of the outer skin layer of the body?

10 In what script is the Russian alphabet written?

ANSWERS

1. An ordinary person who indulges in extravagant daydreaming and fantasies to escape reality. 2. *Animal Farm* (the chief pig). 3. 10. 4. Pork-pie hat. 5. *On Golden Pond*. 6. In vitro fertilization. 7. Vienna. 8. Haslet. 9. Epidermis. 10. Cyrillic.

QUIZ 15

1 In chemistry, what is the term for a particle of matter so small that it cannot be split?

2 Derived from Latin, the term 'caveat emptor' means we should ignore our hunger. True or false?

3 What is the name of a hat that has a shallow crown, a wide brim that is turned up at the back to hold decorative flowers?

4 What is found in the middle of a 'Sussex Pond Pudding'?

5 In music, what other term, apart from 'adagio', means slowly?

6 What is the term given to philosophical discussion and logical disputing?

7 From which animal do we get 'vellum'?

8 What is the name of the branches of the windpipe running into the lungs?

9 Traditionally, to whom is the first toast made at a wedding?

10 What is the title of the operetta that Sullivan composed without Gilbert to a libretto by F. C. Burnand?

ANSWERS

1. Atom. 2. False. It means 'Let the buyer beware'. 3. Watteau hat.
4. A lemon. 5. Lento. 6. Dialectic 7. Calf (cow). 8. Bronchi. 9. To the bride and groom. 10. Cox and Box.

QUIZ 16

• •

1 Dermatology is the medical treatment of blood diseases. True or false?

2 What is the result of alpha decay, beta decay or gamma decay?

3 With how many letters does each player start in a game of 'Scrabble'?

4 In Norse mythology, who slayed the dragon, 'Fafnir'?

5 Which bear in A. A. Milne's books loves honey?

6 What is the name given to the voluntary bureau organization giving advice to people who are uncertain about their rights or who seek special state or voluntary aid but do not know where to find it?

7 What were commissioned by C. Ludwig in 1721?

8 Which British prime minister said 'An iron curtain has descended across the continent'?

9 Of which country is Ottawa the capital?

10 From which fruit is the West Country 'Scrumpy' made?

ANSWERS

1. False. Treatment of skin diseases. 12. Radiation. 3. 7. 4. Sigurd (or Siegfried). 5. 'Winnie-the-Pooh'. 6. Citizens' Advice Bureau. 7. Bach's Brandenburg Concertos. 8. Winston Churchill. 9. Canada. 10. Apples.

QUIZ 17

• •

1 What is the term we use, derived from Latin, which means 'note well or observe'?

2 What breed of cow with dark red or light brown colouring, famous for its rich milk was originally bred on the Channel Islands?

3 Where was 'Mr Orange' first shot in the film Reservoir Dogs?

4 To which area of medicine does paediatrics refer?

5 What is the name of the giants with a single eye in mid-forehead, encountered by Odysseus?

6 What is the capital city of Sudan, known to many British people as the place where General Gordon was killed in the 1880s?

7 What does E-mail stand for?

8 From what is 'scampi' made?

9 For which street is 'Millionaires' Row' a nickname?

10 Which sport is being described by the term 'natation'?

ANSWERS

1. Nota bene. 2. Jersey cow. 3. In the stomach. 4. Treatment of children's diseases. 5. Cyclops. 6. Khartoum. 7. Electronic mail. 8. Prawns. 9. Kensington Palace Gardens. 10. Swimming.

QUIZ 18

- -

1 In tennis, what is the score if each player has scored 40?

2 What is a CV?

3 Name the two most expensive properties in the game of 'Monopoly'?

4 What is your 'alter ego'?

5 What is the name of the highly ornate style of architecture and art that flourished in Europe from the late 16th century to the early 18th century?

6 In 'Scrabble' what does the letter 'W' score?

7 What is the name of the therapy which uses massage and infra-red or ultra-violet rays in its treatment?

8 Who, in one of Jane Austen's novels, was known as a 'match-maker'?

9 What is the Latin phrase we use to say 'by virtue or office or because of one's position'?

10 In which decade were 'Teddy boys' particularly fashionable in Britain?

ANSWERS

1. Deuce. 2. Curriculum Vitae (outline of a person's professional qualifications). 3. Park Lane and Mayfair. 4. Your other self. 5. Baroque. 6. Four. 7. Physiotherapy. 8. 'Emma'. 9. Ex officio. 10. The 1950s.

QUIZ 19

• •

1   What does a sphygmomanometer measure?

2   In golf, what term means a score of one stroke under par for the hole?

3   In Greek mythology, what is the name of the creature having the head, trunk and arms of a man, and the legs of a horse?

4   What is banting?

5   What does WYSIWYG stand for?

6   In which US state is Hollywood situated?

7   What is the name of the alphabet used to clarify individual letters in radio communications?

8   In Lewis Carroll's book Alice's Adventures in Wonderland, who said, 'The Queen of Hearts, she made some tarts, All on a summer day: The Knave of Hearts, he stole those tarts, And took them quite away!'?

9   What species is 'Bombay duck'?

10 Which muscles fill the spaces between the ribs to prevent them being sucked in or blown out during respiration?

ANSWERS

1. Blood pressure. 2. Birdie. 3. Centaur. 4. A method of slimming by eating high amounts of protein and avoiding sugar, starch and fat. 5. What you see is what you get. 6. California. 7. Phonetic alphabet. 8. 'White Rabbit'. 9. Fish. 10. Intercostal muscles.

QUIZ 20

. . . .

1 What does 'vice versa' mean?

2 What is the chemical formula for water?

3 What is a baud?

4 From which mythology does afreet, the powerful evil demon, come?

5 What is the name of Socrates' wife who gave her name to mean an ill-tempered or irritable woman or wife?

6 What do we call a group of whales?

7 What is the common name for the patella?

8 Jack Sprat refused to eat what type of food?

9 What is the fifth book of the Bible?

10 What happened to a 'phoenix', the fabulous bird of classical mythology, when it destroyed itself on a burning altar?

ANSWERS

1. The other way round. 2. H_2O. 3. A unit of measuring the speed of electronic data transmission. 4. Arab mythology. 5. Xanthippe. 6. A school (or gam). 7. Knee-cap. 8. Fat. 9. Deuteronomy. 10. A new bird emerged from the ashes.

QUIZ 21

• •

1 What is a 'post mortem'?

2 In which sport was a 'mashie' used for lifting the ball high?

3 What activity do electromyographs record?

4 What is the full name for CO_2?

5 What is the name of the fine, soft, sheer fabric of plain weave used especially in shirts, lingerie, dresses and handkerchiefs?

6 What does the Beaufort Scale measure?

7 How many pints of beer are there in a 'hogshead'?

8 What is the name for a plant that has resulted from crossing two different species?

9 Who, in 1882, said 'Our market is the world'?

10 What is the capital of Luxembourg?

ANSWERS

1. An examination of a corpse to discover the cause of death. 2. Golf.
3. Muscle activity. 4. Carbon dioxide. 5. Batiste. 6. Wind speed. 7. 432.
8. Hybrid. 9. Henry Heinz. 10. Luxembourg (City).

QUIZ 22

1　What do we call a young horse?

2　Which town is the capital of Jamaica?

3　What is the most frequently used letter in English?

4　In his play The Rehearsal, who wrote; 'The object of art is to give life a shape'?

5　On Easter Sunday, what cake is traditionally eaten?

6　In the card games bridge or whist, what is the name for a hand in which none of the cards is higher than nine?

7　What is the musical term for a composition, usually on a religious theme, for voices and orchestra?

8　Who are 'Athos, Porthos and Aramis' in a novel by Dumas?

9　What is the square diagonally opposite 'Go' in the game of 'Monopoly'?

10　In the game 'Triominoes', what shape are all the pieces?

ANSWERS

1. Foal. 2. Kingston. 3. E. 4. Jean Anouilh. 5. Simnel cake. 6. Yarborough.
7. Oratorio. 8. The Three Musketeers. 9. 'Free Parking'. 10. Triangles.

QUIZ 23

• •

1 What is the fifth letter of the Greek alphabet?

2 What three layers make up 'Millionaire's Shortcake'?

3 What is a person's 'alma mater'?

4 What fruit is used to flavour Aurum liqueur?

5 The finger and toe nails of the human body have nerves and blood vessels. True or false?

6 What, in musical terms, is a rhapsody?

7 What, in Britain, are traditionally eaten on Good Friday?

8 Who plays the part of 'Ed Wood' in the film of the same name?

9 How many squares are there in total on a chess board?

10 What is a 'non sequitur'?

ANSWERS

1. Epsilon. 2. Shortcake, caramel, chocolate. 3. One's school, college, university, etc. 4. Orange. 5. False. 6. A work with no set form, often based on folk tunes. 7. Hot Cross Buns. 8. Johnny Depp. 9. 64. 10. Something that does not logically follow from what has gone before.

QUIZ 24

1 Who wrote The Mayor of Casterbridge?

2 Ozone is a highly toxic, unstable, colourless gas. True or false?

3 Which are generally hotter, green or red chillies?

4 In one of his essays, who is quoted as writing, 'The remedy is worse than the disease'?

5 What musical term means a composition in which a refrain is repeated between separate sections?

6 As opposed to a 'tied house', what is the name given to a pub that is free to receive its supplies from a number of brewers?

7 In Dickens' novel, what is the hero, Chuzzlewit's, first name?

8 What does the abbreviation p.m. stand for?

9 How many pawns does each player have in the game of 'Chess'?

10 What does it mean to 'bowdlerize a book'?

ANSWERS

1. Thomas Hardy. 2. True. 3. Green. 4. Francis Bacon (1st Baron Verulam).
5. Rondo. 6. 'Free house'. 7. 'Martin'. 8. Post meridiem (in the afternoon).
9. Eight. 10. To remove all the words or passages that are considered indecent.

QUIZ 25

• •

1 According to some alchemists, into what was the 'philosopher's stone' thought to be capable of transmuting base metals?

2 In which country is the port of Antwerp?

3 What spirit is made from potatoes?

4 From which country did chocolate originate?

5 In the Bible, who was thrown into the lion's den?

6 What was the name of the spoilt ill-tempered orphan in Frances Hodgson Burnett's The Secret Garden?

7 How many rooks are there on the board at the start of a game of chess?

8 Where are the Crown Jewels displayed when not being used?

9 What is a 'modus operandi'?

10 In which film did Rhett Butler fall in love with Vivienne Leigh?

ANSWERS

1. Gold. 2. Belgium. 3. Vodka. 4. Mexico. 5. Daniel. 6. 'Mary'. 7. Four. 8. Tower of London. 9. A way of working, a procedure. 10. Gone With The Wind.

QUIZ 26

1 Into which sea does the River Mersey flow?

2 In what part of the body is the tibia found?

3 In which group of islands is Tenerife?

4 What is frangipane?

5 Who said 'That's one small step for man, one giant leap for mankind'?

6 Which type of tree is a traditional Christmas tree?

7 Which of George Eliot's heros was a single, adopted father?

8 What do we mean when we use the term 'et al'?

9 What alcoholic beverage is commonly associated with a variety of the card game 'Rummy'?

10 What is the character name of the waitress in the original Fawlty Towers TV series?

ANSWERS

1. Irish Sea. 2. Leg (thigh). 3. Canary Islands. 4. Almond-flavoured paste (for cakes). 5. Neil Armstrong (of his first step onto the moon). 6. Fir tree. 7. 'Silas Marner'. 8. And others. 9. Gin. 10. 'Polly'.

QUIZ 27

• •

1 What musical term means 'notes of a chord played in quick succession'?

2 The term National Debt was first used in 1694. How much was it then?

3 Who provides the voice for the starring child in Look Who's Talking?

4 What is the name of the Scottish ball game similar to hockey?

5 What do the letters RSVP stand for?

6 What do 'gorgons', in classical mythology, have for hair?

7 What is a Bailey bridge?

8 What name do we give to a marinated herring?

9 What is the name of the American comic strip orphan character who gets into a lot of trouble especially when 'Daddy Warbucks' is away?

10 Which bird was the emblem of the Roman Empire?

ANSWERS

1. Arpeggio. 2. £49 million. 3. Bruce Willis. 4. Shinty. 5. Répondez s'il vous plaît (please reply, used at the end of an invitation). 6. Serpents. 7. A kind of temporary military bridge. 8. Rollmop. 9. 'Little Orphan Annie'. 10. Eagle.

QUIZ 28

• •

1 Which French writer in his book The Fall is quoted 'Style, like sheer silk, too often hides eczema'?

2 What is a 'chihuahua'?

3 What is the more common name given to 'Silver Darlings' which live in British waters?

4 Taken from Dickens' novel A Christmas Carol, what term have we coined to mean a miser?

5 What is a 'golden handshake'?

6 What nationality was the musician 'Liberace'?

7 What, in music, is a prelude?

8 By what military display is the official birthday of the sovereign marked?

9 To what did Tom Hanks liken life in the film Forrest Gump?

10 Name the sport played between two teams of players on horseback?

ANSWERS

1. Albert Camus. 2. Dog (Mexican dwarf dog). 3. Herring. 4. Scrooge.
5. A large sum of money given to certain employees when they leave a company after a long period of service. 6. American. 7. A piece introducing a larger work; a show-piece for piano and orchestra. 8. Trooping the colour.
9. 'A box of chocolates'. 10. 'Polo'.

QUIZ 29

. . . .

1 In music, 'nocturne' suggests the qualities of what time of day?

2 Which Spanish writer in his novel Don Quixote, is quoted as saying, 'Tell me what company thou keepest, and I'll tell thee what thou art'?

3 What type of food is Brin D'Affinois?

4 By what name was Sri Lanka formerly known?

5 What is the ingredient that is usually used to turn rice or curry yellow?

6 Who wrote the play The Merry Wives of Windsor?

7 What does the abbreviation a.m. stand for?

8 What parts of the body do orthopaedics treat?

9 What drink named after a bartender consists of gin, lime (or lemon) juice, sugar and soda water?

10 What is the name of the winged horse, offspring of Gorgon Medusa, and the mount of Perseus and Bellerophon?

ANSWERS

1. Night. 2. Miguel de Cervantes. 3. Cheese. 4. Ceylon. 5. Turmeric.
6. William Shakespeare. 7. Ante meridiem (in the morning). 8. Bone and muscles. 9. Tom Collins. 10. 'Pegasus'.

QUIZ 30

1. When was Braille invented? (a) 1824, (b) 1799 or (c) 1856?

2. What name is given to the chief muscle of the hip forming the curve of the buttocks?

3. Which French president who came to power in 1969 has a museum in Paris named after him?

4. What, in the Arabian legend, is a 'roc'?

5. In 'Scrabble' what does the letter 'B' score?

6. For what does the abbreviation ad stand?

7. What is the term for the treatment of women's diseases?

8. What is the full name given to the arrangement of the chemical elements?

9. What is the eponymic name of the visible projection at the front of the neck, formed by the thyroid cartilage?

10. Which shrub-like plant produces the berries to make gin?

ANSWERS

1. (a) 1824. 2. Glutens maximus. 3. Georges Pompidou. 4. A bird of enormous size. 5. Three. 6. Anno Domini: in the year of our Lord. 7. Gynaecology. 8. The Periodic Table of Elements. 9. Adam's apple. 10. Juniper.

QUIZ 31

. . . .

1   Where is the Scottish Football Cup Final played?

2   Which vegetable did Mark Twain call 'cabbage with a college education'?

3   Of what are 'venules' the smallest branches?

4   What is the name for the under layer of skin (beneath the epidermis)?

5   From which animal do we get 'cat gut'?

6   What is the musical term for a study, a piece designed as an exercise?

7   Who said of Prime Minister Gladstone, 'He speaks to me as if I was a public meeting'?

8   What food was originally used by the Aztecs as currency?

9   What shape is farfale pasta?

10 Who was the British General who began the Scouts Association?

ANSWERS

1. Hampden Park. 2. Cauliflower. 3. Veins. 4. Corium or dermis. 5. Sheep, horse or ass. 6. Étude. 7. Queen Victoria. 8. Cocoa beans. 9. Bows. 10. Lord Robert Baden-Powell.

QUIZ 32

• •

1 What is the term for the type of tree which annually sheds its leaves?

2 What are sturgeon's eggs also known as?

3 Which character said 'I am a bear of very little brain, and long words bother me'?

4 Which salary scale for teachers was established in 1924 and abolished in 1987?

5 From which fruit is calvados made?

6 Which 19th century author said 'There are three kinds of lies: lies, damned lies, and statistics'?

7 Which forgotten composer had his music re-introduced to the public by Mendelssohn?

8 Which moustache which was especially popular with men in the British Air Force in World War II, is long and heavy and curves upwards at both ends?

9 What is the name given to the undeveloped, slightly sunken growth buds on potatoes?

10 In which country is Lake Como?

ANSWERS

1. Deciduous. 2. Caviar. 3. 'Winnie the Pooh'. 4. Burnham Scale. 5. Apples.
6. Mark Twain. 7. J. S. Bach. 8. Handlebar moustache. 9. Eye. 10. Italy.

QUIZ 33

• •

1   To which college in Cambridge does the Bridge of Sighs belong?

2   What does 'persona non grata' mean?

3   In the nursery rhyme, who sat in a corner eating Christmas pie?

4   What does the term 'heeling in' mean, in gardening?

5   Which famous Christian preacher said, 'I look upon the world as my parish'?

6   What is the gelling agent in jelly?

7   In which city was the first public performance of Handel's Messiah?

8   What are Dr Martens?

9   What is the capital of Lebanon?

10 According to tradition, where must a true Cockney be born to be so called?

ANSWERS

1. St John's College. 2. A person unacceptable or not welcome. 3. 'Little Jack Horner'. 4. Temporary planting (especially fruit trees). 5. John Wesley.
6. Gelatine. 7. Dublin. 8. A make of strong, heavy boots with laces. 9. Beirut.
10. Within the sound of the Bow Bells.

QUIZ 34

• •

1 What is the English name for the American game of 'checkers'?

2 In 'loco parentis' means that one has eccentric parents. True or false?

3 Which 20th century author, in one of his novels, wrote 'All animals are equal, but some animals are more equal than others'?

4 What is the raising agent used in soda bread?

5 Traditionally, on which day are pancakes eaten?

6 What is the name for a shirt with short sleeves and a collar, made out of soft, knitted cotton material?

7 What is the name of the joint on a stem from which leaves arise?

8 What scale of values measures soil alkalinity or acidity?

9 Of which country is Tripoli the capital?

10 What is the name for the bells of the London church St Mary-le-Bow?

ANSWERS

1. Draughts. 2. False. It means in the place or role of a parent. 3. George Orwell. 4. Bicarbonate of Soda. 5. Shrove Tuesday. 6. Polo shirt. 7. Node. 8. pH level. 9. Libya. 10. Bow Bells.

QUIZ 35

. . . .

1 Which British statesman is quoted in various speeches as saying: 'Wait and see'?

2 For what is arrowroot most commonly used?

3 What is the American word for English 'crisps'?

4 How many letters are there in the Greek alphabet?

5 From what region of France does Claret come?

6 Which British statesman said, 'A Conservative government is an organized hypocrisy'?

7 In one of his essays, who is quoted as saying, 'Money is like muck, not good except it be spread'?

8 What is the English word for the American 'fall'?

9 Who composed the songs 'The Old Folks at Home' and 'Camptown Races'?

10 What colour does beta carotene turn food?

ANSWERS

1. Herbert Henry Asquith. 2. Thickening. 3. Chips. 4. 24. 5. Bordeaux.
6. Benjamin Disraeli. 7. Francis Bacon (1st Baron Verulam). 8. Autumn.
9. Stephen Foster. 10. Orange.

QUIZ 36

. . . .

1 What kind of plant is marjoram?

2 The people of which religion follow the teaching of Siddhartha Gantama?

3 In which country is Sevastapol?

4 'Little Jack Horner sat in the corner, eating…' Finish this line of the nursery rhyme.

5 What drink is made from molasses?

6 Who is said to have confessed, 'Give me chastity and continence, but not yet'?

7 In music, what is 'The 48'?

8 In which play by Oscar Wilde did 'Lord Darlington' say, 'I can resist everything except temptation'?

9 In the world of pop music, which brothers 'Walked Right Back'?

10 In one of Jane Austen's novels, who is quoted as saying, 'One half of the world cannot understand the pleasures of the other'?

ANSWERS

1. Herb. 2. Buddhists. 3. Ukraine. 4. a Christmas pie. 5. Rum. 6. Saint Augustine. 7. The name given to J. S. Bach's collection of 48 Preludes and Fugues in 'The Well-Tempered Clavier'. 8. Lady Windermere's Fan. 9. The Everly Brothers. 10. Emma.

QUIZ 37

. . . .

1 From whom does the teddy bear take its name?

2 In which George Orwell novel is 'Big Brother' said to be watching you?

3 On which musical instrument would you be most likely to play a pibroch?

4 What is the name of the brimless Scottish cap, which usually has a pom-pom on top?

5 In the song which line follows 'Rule Britannia, Britannia rules the waves'?

6 Who lost her sheep in the traditional nursery rhyme?

7 In which country is Marrakesh?

8 To which religion do 'Sangha' monks and nuns belong?

9 In the song, who stuck a feather in his cap and called it macaroni?

10 What do we call the drink which is made from the roots of the Smilax plant?

ANSWERS

1. Theodore Roosevelt (US president). 2. 1984. 3. Bagpipes. 4. Tam-o'-shanter. 5. 'Britons never, never, never shall be slaves'. 6. 'Little Bo-Peep'. 7. Morocco. 8. Buddhism. 9. 'Yankee Doodle'. 10. Sarsaparilla.

QUIZ 38

• •

1 What is the French term used for a clear soup?

2 Who in the Bible said:'What is truth?'?

3 What kind of fruit is a pearmain?

4 What does an epicure enjoy?

5 What is the American name for the game 'noughts and crosses'?

6 Which tree is associated with Lebanon?

7 What is the common name for the trachea?

8 Who, in Jane Austen's Pride and Prejudice said,'I have been a selfish being all my life, in practice, though not in principle'?

9 What is a canapé?

10 In which musical are there two gangs called the 'Sharks' and the 'Jets'?

ANSWERS

1. Consommé. 2. Pilate. 3. Apple. 4. Good food and drink (good living).
5. Tick-tack-toe. 6. Cedar. 7. Windpipe. 8. Mr Darcy. 9. A small piece of toast. with a savoury topping. 10. West Side Story.

QUIZ 39

• •

1 For what purpose, in the nursery rhyme, did 'Jack and Jill' go up the hill?

2 What is the name given to the soft felt hat with an indented crown?

3 If you were playing a jew's harp, how would you be holding it?

4 From which Jane Austen novel is the quotation, 'Happiness in marriage is entirely a matter of chance' taken?

5 What kind of drink is porter?

6 What is the name for the mass of spongy tissue between the back of the nose and throat?

7 What state of being do Buddhists hope to achieve through regular meditation?

8 Having a holiday in Valletta, in which country would you be?

9 What is the American word for the Engish spring onion?

10 Which Spanish musical instrument is made of two wooden shells?

ANSWERS

1. To fetch a pail of water. 2. Trilby. 3. In your teeth. 4. *Pride and Prejudice*.
5. Dark, bitter beer. 6. Adenoid. 7. Nirvana. 8. Malta. 9. Scallion.
10. Castanets.

QUIZ 40

• •

1   What is the American word for English 'sweets'?

2   In the nursery rhyme 'Ding dong bell', who put Pussy in the well?

3   In criminal terms, if someone is 'incarcerated', where are they?

4   What musical instrument would a timpanist play?

5   What type of competitor races in the 'St Leger'?

6   Which American president said: 'Think of your forefathers! Think of your posterity'?

7   From which language do the following come: 'fjord', 'ski', 'slalom'?

8   In music, which note follows 'soh'?

9   Who said, 'Give me a firm place to stand, and I will move the earth'?

10 According to the proverb, what part of clouds are silver?

ANSWERS

1. Candy. 2. 'Little Johnny Green'. 3. In prison. 4. Drums (percussion instruments). 5. Horses. 6. John Quincy Adams. 7. Norwegian. 8. Lah. 9. Archimedes. 10. Linings.

QUIZ 41

• •

1 In the nursery rhyme, 'I had a little nut tree', it would only bear two things, what were they?

2 Which scale is commonly used to measure the magnitude of earthquakes?

3 What is the English word for American 'pants'?

4 Of what is a 'tintinnabulation' the sound?

5 Which county is particularly associated with the song 'On Ilkley Moor baht 'at'?

6 'Mother's Ruin' is a nickname for which drink?

7 From which main ingredient is sauerkraut made?

8 Who originally said, 'The woman that deliberates is lost'?

9 Which musical instrument is a national emblem of Eire?

10 In criminal terms, what does it mean to 'purloin' something?

ANSWERS

1. A silver nutmeg and a golden pear. 2. Richter scale. 3. Trousers. 4. Ringing bells. 5. Yorkshire. 6. Gin. 7. Cabbage. 8. Joseph Addison. 9. Harp. 10. Steal something.

QUIZ 42

• •

1. What are you doing if you 'pull the wool over someone's eyes'?

2. If a picture is painted 'monochromatically', how is it painted?

3. What word do we get from Ambrose Everett Burnside, referring to our hair?

4. In his fable The Jay and the Peacock, who wrote, 'It is not only fine feathers that make fine birds'?

5. What does 'long in the tooth mean'?

6. Which type of meat is correctly used to make Wiener Schnitzel?

7. What is sold by a 'costermonger'?

8. From which language do the words 'caviar', 'kaftan' and 'kiosk' originate?

9. What is the name of the Muslim's annual month of fasting?

10. 'Hey diddle diddle, the cat and the fiddle, the…' Finish the line of this nursery rhyme.

ANSWERS

1. Deceiving or tricking someone. 2. In black and white, in one colour or different shades of one colour. 3. Sideburns. 4. Aesop. 5. Getting old. 6. Veal. 7. Fruit and/or vegetables. 8. Turkish. 9. Ramadan. 10. '…cow jumped over the moon'.

QUIZ 43

• •

1 What flavour is Crème de Menthe?

2 'Goosey goosey gander, Whither shall I wander, Upstairs and downstairs, And in…' Finish the line of this nursery rhyme.

3 What do we commonly call the thyroid cartilage in the neck when it is particularly prominent in men?

4 What is a 'laptop'?

5 During World War II, which vegetable did the Ministry of Food encourage people to eat to help them see in the dark?

6 What kind of food is gazpacho?

7 Who wrote the fable from which the term 'cry wolf' comes?

8 What does a 'cartographer' draw?

9 From what main ingredients is bubble and squeak usually made?

10 What is the familiar name of the medallion awarded annually for distinguished achievement in American theatre, named after the actress Antoinette Perry?

ANSWERS

1. Peppermint. 2. 'My lady's chamber'. 3. Adam's apple. 4. Portable computer. 5. Carrots. 6. Soup (cold). 7. Aesop. 8. Maps. 9. Boiled cabbage, potatoes and sometimes meat. 10. 'Tony'.

QUIZ 44

1 What does 'heterogeneous' mean?

2 In which country would you take a holiday in Paphos?

3 Whose name is remembered for the closure of many British railway lines in the 1960s?

4 In which book of the Bible are the Ten Commandments first listed?

5 What does 'donkey's years' mean?

6 At least once in their lives, Muslims must try to make a pilgrimage to which holy city?

7 In the 1997 film Titanic who starred with Leonardo DiCaprio?

8 Of what is 'choux' a type?

9 Who was the sole prisoner in a German jail for 21 years?

10 Proverbially, who should we not teach to suck eggs?

ANSWERS

1. Varied, consisting of unlike people or things. 2. Cyprus. 3. Richard Beeching. 4. Exodus. 5. A long time. 6. Mecca. 7. Kate Winslet. 8. Pastry. 9. Rudolf Hess. 10. Grandmother.

QUIZ 45

• •

1   In the nursery rhyme, who tried to put 'Humpty Dumpty' together again?

2   Which herb also gives its name to a wise teacher, deeply respected for his experience and judgment?

3   Who was the first chancellor of the German Empire?

4   What is the English word for an American hobo?

5   Where are you living if you are living in 'cloud cuckoo land'?

6   To which French art movement did the artist Monet belong?

7   What is the name of the most massive tree in the world?

8   In the Bible, in the book of Genesis what did God create on the fifth day?

9   In which children's comic does 'Dennis the Menace' feature?

10 How many vowels altogether are there in the Russian alphabet?

ANSWERS

1. 'All the king's horses and all the king's men'. 2. Sage. 3. Otto von Bismarck.
4. Tramp. 5. An imaginary fantasy world. 6. Impressionism. 7. Giant Sequoia.
8. Animal life in the sea and air. 9. The Beano. 10. Ten.

QUIZ 46

● ●

1. What kind of seafood are 'Moules à la Marinière'?

2. 'Hickory dickory dock, The mouse ran up the clock, The clock struck…' What did the clock strike?

3. In which year did the Battle of Agincourt take place?

4. What two types of 'palate' are there in the mouth?

5. According to the proverb, at what will a drowning man clutch?

6. What is the American word for a fringe (of hair)?

7. Who was the leader of the 'Free French' forces during World War II?

8. What colour is angelica?

9. What six parts of the body must a Muslim wash before they pray?

10. According to Benjamin Franklin, what makes a man healthy, wealthy and wise?

ANSWERS

1. Mussels. 2. One. 3. 1415. 4. Soft and hard palates. 5. A straw. 6. Bangs. 7. Charles de Gaulle. 8. Green. 9. Wash their hands, face, head, arms, legs and feet. 10. Early to bed and early to rise.

QUIZ 47

. . . .

1   Which two continents does the Bosphorus link?

2   What was the name of the toy spaceman in Toy Story?

3   Which US political party has the nickname 'Grand Old Party'?

4   Who was the author of 'The Thirty-Nine Steps'?

5   At which battle was General Custer defeated in 1876?

6   What are the three primary colours?

7   From which quiz programme does the phrase 'Your starter for 10' come?

8   Whose Modern English Usage was first published in 1926?

9   What is the US term for a 'big wheel'?

10 What do the initials ISA stand for?

ANSWERS

1. Europe and Asia. 2. 'Buzz Lightyear'. 3. Republican Party. 4. John Buchan.
5. Little Bighorn. 6. Red, yellow and blue. 7. University Challenge. 8. Henry
Watson Fowler. 9. A ferris wheel. 10. Individual Savings Account.

QUIZ 48

- -

1 Who was the first woman prime minister of Britain?

2 Who wrote the book Pilgrim's Progress?

3 On what play was the musical My Fair Lady based?

4 The word 'metamorphose' means (a) to change into a different form; (b) to become dead; or (c) to fly into the sky?

5 Mills and Boon is famous for publishing what kind of books?

6 In the Bible what was the name of the woman who was a prophet and judge of Israel?

7 Who wrote A Brief History of Time?

8 What was the profession of Frank Lloyd Wright?

9 Who invented the idea of lateral thinking?

10 In which Scottish lake is a monster said to live?

ANSWERS

1. Margaret Thatcher. 2. John Bunyan. 3. Pygmalion. 4. (a) to change into a different form. 5. Stories about love and romance. 6. Deborah. 7. Stephen Hawking. 8. Architect. 9. Edward de Bono. 10. Loch Ness.

QUIZ 49

. . . .

1   From what main ingredient is hummus made?

2   For which fruit is Seville famous?

3   In which year did the Automobile Association launch its 'Relay' service?

4   Charles II of England, Scotland and Ireland, died in which year?

5   Who coined the phrase: A country 'fit for heroes to live in'?

6   What is the name of the Israeli parliament?

7   What do the initials CBI stand for?

8   What was the name of the groups of women who, in the early 20th century, tried to gain for women the right to vote?

9   Who became known as 'Saint Mugg'?

10 What cheese is traditionally eaten with Christmas cake?

ANSWERS

1. Chick peas. 2. Oranges. 3. 1973. 4. 1685. 5. Lloyd George. 6. The Knesset. 7. Confederation of British Industry. 8. The Suffragettes. 9. Malcolm Muggeridge. 10. Stilton cheese.

QUIZ 50

• •

1 Who wrote the Just So Stories?

2 Who wrote the novel The Corridors of Power?

3 What is the French name for chicken casserole with red wine?

4 Who is the chairman of Microsoft?

5 In which year did Vasco da Gama discover the sea route from Portugal to India, around the Cape of Good Hope?

6 Which US state lies between Illinois and Ohio?

7 In which year was the play Look Back in Anger first presented?

8 Which designer and businessman founded the Habitat stores?

9 Which character in David Copperfield by Charles Dickens was known for being 'ever so umble'?

10 From which language do the words 'álgebra' and 'alcohol' originate?

ANSWERS

1. Rudyard Kipling. 2. C. P. Snow. 3. Coq-au-vin. 4. Bill Gates. 5. 1498.
6. Indiana. 7. 1956. 8. Terence Conran. 9. 'Uriah Heep'. 10. Arabic.

QUIZ 51

1 In which year did Adenauer become Chancellor of West Germany?

2 Proverbially, who should we be careful not to empty out along with the bath water?

3 The phrase 'Not a lot of people know that' was made famous by whom?

4 What does the Russian word 'perestroika' mean?

5 Who wrote War and Peace?

6 From which language do the words 'geisha', 'rickshaw' and 'kamikaze' originate?

7 Which TV interviewer, who interviewed politicians, was famous for wearing a bow tie with spots on it?

8 What do the initials CAD stand for?

9 What is the Burrell collection in Glasgow?

10 Who did Margaret Thatcher follow as leader of the Conservative party?

ANSWERS

1. 1949. 2. The baby. 3. Michael Caine. 4. Restructuring. 5. Leo Tolstoy.
6. Japanese. 7. Sir Robin Day. 8. Computer aided design. 9. An art collection. 10. Ted Heath.

QUIZ 52

· ·

1   What kind of soup is bouillabaisse?

2   How many vowels are there in the Greek alphabet?

3   What do you do when you 'twist someone's arm'?

4   What kind of region does 'tundra' describe?

5   According to the proverb, what should not be washed in public?

6   Which American president coined the phrase, 'The buck stops here'?

7   What does 'ad infinitum' mean?

8   'Sub rosa' is Latin for beautifully. True or false?

9   What mark is used to show that a product meets the traditional safety standards of the British Standards Institution?

10 To which genus do cabbages belong?

ANSWERS

1. Fish. 2. 7. 3. Persuade someone to do something. 4. Rolling, treeless plain of arctic region (particularly Russia). 5. Dirty linen. 6. Harry S. Truman. 7. Endlessly. 8. False. It means secretly or confidentially. 9. Kite-mark. 10. Brassica.

QUIZ 53

• •

1 According to the proverb, what is as good as a feast?

2 What is Adam's Ale?

3 Which of Shakespeare's plays involves a pound of flesh?

4 Of what is 'Meaux' a type?

5 What is the capital of Algeria?

6 What is 'terra firma'?

7 Which ingredient gives the flavour to Amaretto liqueurs and biscuits?

8 Who, in the play The Importance of Being Earnest, said 'to lose one parent, Mr Worthing, may be regarded as a misfortune; to lose both looks like carelessness'?

9 On which bird is a parson's nose found?

10 Where is the Derby horse race held?

ANSWERS

1. Enough. 2. Water. 3. The Merchant of Venice. 14. Mustard. 5. Algiers.
6. Solid ground. 7. Almond. 8. 'Lady Bracknell'. 14. Chicken. 10. Epsom.

QUIZ 54

. . . .

1   In 1869 which major engineering feat linking two seas was opened?

2   Which novelist wrote Tinker, Tailor, Soldier, Spy?

3   What were accidentally discovered in some jars in Jordan in 1947?

4   In the nursery rhyme 'Georgie Porgie, pudding and pie', when did Georgie Porgie run away?

5   In which year did Kellog's launch their cereal product 'Rice Krispies'?

6   What is the traditional name for the day after Christmas Day?

7   In what script is the English alphabet written?

8   Traditionally, who proposes a toast to the parents of the bride and groom at a wedding?

9   What is the grammatical term used to say a roundabout way of expressing something?

10 Where did Weber establish a theatre for the performance of opera in German?

ANSWERS

1. The Suez Canal. 2. John le Carré. 3. The Dead Sea Scrolls. 4. When the boys came out to play. 5. 1929. 6. Boxing Day. 7. Roman. 8. The best man. 14. Periphrasis. 10. Dresden.

QUIZ 55

. . . .

1 In which year did the 'Great Train Robbery' take place?

2 Whose last words were, 'Get my swan costume ready'?

3 For which traditional dish is 'pilau' an accompaniment?

4 How many 'tarsal' bones do we have in each foot?

5 What are the surnames of 'Romeo' and 'Juliet' in Shakespeare's play Romeo and Juliet?

6 By what other name was Richard I known?

7 What is the name of the thin, curling outgrowths by which certain climbing plants cling to supports?

8 In which country is Lake Bala found?

9 What do we play with two fingers on the piano, but Borodin, Rimsky-Korskov and Liszt composed variations of?

10 What is the name for the chest cavity?

ANSWERS

1. 1963. 2. Anna Pavlova, the Russian ballerina. 3. Curry (pilau rice). 4. 7.
5. 'Montague' and 'Capulet'. 6. Richard the Lionheart. 7. Tendril. 8. Wales.
9. 'Chopsticks'. 10. Thorax.

QUIZ 56

. . . .

1 What is the special name for the caller who calls people to prayer from the top of a mosque in Muslim countries?

2 The famous 'To be or not to be' speech is in which Shakespeare play?

3 What is the English word for an American 'sedan'?

4 Who invented the pneumatic bicycle tyre in 1888?

5 What does to 'get someone's goat' mean?

6 Who was the drummer in The Beatles?

7 What is the English word for the American 'half note'?

8 How many characters are there in the Russian alphabet?

9 What is the name of the channel leading to the eardrum?

10 What is the American word for grilling (food)?

ANSWERS

1. Muezzin. 2. Hamlet. 3. Saloon (car). 4. John Dunlop. 5. To annoy or irritate someone. 6. Ringo Starr. 7. Minim. 8. 33. 9. Eustachian tube. 10. Broiling.

QUIZ 57

1 In which year did President de Gaulle veto UK membership of the European Economic Community?

2 The 'Mappa Mundi' is displayed at which English cathedral?

3 The actress Norma Jean Baker is better known as who?

4 Who is famous for his weekly Letter from America?

5 Where does the phrase 'a fly in the ointment' come from?

6 What is the fruit of a certain type of Rose?

7 From which Jane Austen novel is 'Let other pens dwell on guilt and misery' quoted?

8 What is the American word for 'nappy'?

9 With which country do you associate the drink Pernod?

10 Which song begins, 'Dashing through the snow, in a one horse open sleigh'?

ANSWERS

1. 1963. 2. Hereford. 3. Marilyn Monroe. 4. Alistair Cooke. 5. The Bible, Ecclesiastes. 6. Hips. 7. Mansfield Park. 8. Diaper. 9. France. 10. 'Jingle Bells'.

QUIZ 58

. . . .

1   What is another name for the Decalogue?

2   What is the name of the mountain face in the USA into which the faces of four US presidents have been carved?

3   For what did Bertrand Russell receive the Nobel Prize in 1950?

4   What is the capital of Spain?

5   In Star Trek 'Mr Spock' comes from which planet?

6   'Ladybird, ladybird, fly away home, Your house is on fire, and…' Finish the line of this nursery rhyme.

7   What is the metric unit of magnetic flux density named after a Croatian-born American electrician?

8   From which country does the drink Ouzo come?

9   On which French river are the ports of Le Havre and Rouen?

10 According to the proverb, of what will you repent at leisure?

ANSWERS

1. The Ten Commandments. 2. Mount Rushmore. 3. Literature. 4. Madrid.
5. Vulcan. 6. '…your children all gone'. 7. Tesla. 8. Greece. 9. Seine.
10. Marrying in haste.

QUIZ 59

1 In which year was the Battle of Bosworth Field?

2 Monday is named after the Moon. True or false?

3 What is the name of the long, narrow lengths of paper sometimes thrown in the US to greet famous people?

4 What do the initials SALT stand for?

5 Who was the main introducer of the TV programme That's Life?

6 Of which country is Nairobi the capital?

7 What is the name for the process of building up and breaking down foodstuffs by the body cells?

8 According to the proverb, what proves the rule?

9 Which capital city stands on the River Tiber?

10 What is the name of the six-pointed star frequently used as the Jewish symbol?

ANSWERS

1. 1485. 2. True. 3. Tickertape. 4. Strategic Arms Limitation Talks.
5. Esther Rantzen. 6. Kenya. 7. Metabolism. 8. The exception. 9. Rome.
10. Star of David.

QUIZ 60

1 In which year is Middle English said to have ended -- the year in which printing was introduced in England by William Caxton?

2 From which folk song does the phrase 'Uncle Tom Cobbleigh and all' come?

3 According to tradition, what social act takes place beneath mistletoe at Christmas?

4 Which dynasty ruled China from 1368 to 1644?

5 What is thremmatology?

6 Who was the founder of Methodism?

7 Complete the book title, Men are from Mars, Women are…?

8 Which seasoning is made from the cayenne plant?

9 Named after an American hat-maker, what is a wide-brimmed, high-crowned felt hat called?

10 In which century was the Hanseatic League first founded?

ANSWERS

1. 1476. 2. Widdicombe Fair. 3. Kissing. 4. The Ming Dynasty. 5. The science of breeding domestic animals and plants. 6. John Wesley. 7. From Venus. 8. Pepper. 9. Stetson. 10. 13th century.

QUIZ 61

1 What is the pseudonym of Herman Cyril McNeile, creator of Hugh 'Bulldog' Drummond?

2 What is the American English name for the boot of a car?

3 Who wrote Robinson Crusoe?

4 What was the name of the Jewish girl who became known for her diary written in hiding during World War II?

5 Which novel, by the American writer Ira Levin, was made into a film in 1968?

6 What is the American word for English 'treacle'?

7 What did Baron Paul Julius von Reuter found?

8 According to the proverb, whose house is his castle?

9 What is the name of a Jewish boy's coming of age?

10 According to a song, to where in Ireland is it a long way?

ANSWERS

1. Sapper. 2. Trunk. 3. Daniel Defoe. 4. Anne Frank. 5. Rosemary's Baby.
6. Molasses. 7. The first news agency. 8. An Englishman's. 9. Bar Mitzvah.
10. Tipperary.

QUIZ 62

1 In which year did women sit on a coroner's jury for the first time?

2 OO, HO and N are all types of what?

3 Which US state is south of Kentucky?

4 Proverbially, if we do not spread the risk, what have we put in one basket?

5 Of which country is Buenos Aires the capital?

6 In which European country is the port of Bergen?

7 What is meant by a 'ballpark figure'?

8 On what night is Hallowe'en?

9 What do the initials CAP stand for?

10 In December 1936 King Edward VIII abdicated in order to marry who?

ANSWERS

1. 1933. 2. Model railway gauges. 3. Tennessee. 4. All our eggs. 5. Argentina.
6. Norway. 7. A rough estimate. 8. 31 October. 9. Common Agricultural
Policy. 10. Mrs Wallis Simpson.

QUIZ 63

. . . .

1 Who wrote Home Thoughts from Abroad?

2 In which European country is the city of Strasbourg?

3 From which language do the words 'harem' and 'carafe' originate?

4 From what family of vegetables does the haricot come?

5 In which town was the comedian Eric Sykes born?

6 Who is said to have said 'Doctor Livingstone, I presume?'

7 What do the letters HMV stand for?

8 Who wrote the book The Compleat Angler?

9 In which year did Amy Johnson fly solo from England to Australia?

10 A samizdat is (a) a Russian tea urn, (b) secret printing and publishing in the Soviet Union, or (c) a Turkish long range weapon?

ANSWERS

1. Robert Browning. 2. France. 3. Arabic. 4. Bean. 5. Oldham. 6. Henry Morton Stanley, at the end of his search for the missionary David Livingstone in the heart of Africa. 7. His Master's Voice. 8. Izaak Walton. 9. 1930. 10. (b) secret printing and publishing in the Soviet Union.

QUIZ 64

• •

1 Which US state lies between California and Utah?

2 In which year was the St Lawrence Seaway completed?

3 According to a famous speech by Shakespeare, how many ages of man are there?

4 What is the more common French name for zucchini?

5 Who partners Richard Madeley on daytime television?

6 In which year did Buddy Holly die?

7 Who coined the phrase 'A little learning is a dangerous thing'?

8 Which Chinese philosopher is sometimes referred to when giving wise advice?

9 Who was the first woman member of a British cabinet?

10 What kind of creature is a skink?

ANSWERS

1. Nevada. 2. 1959. 3 Seven. 4. Courgette. 5. Judy Finnigan. 6. 1959.
7. Alexander Pope. 8. Confucius. 9. Margaret Bondfield (1929). 10. A lizard.

QUIZ 65

• •

1 What acronym describes the type of sleep associated with dreaming?

2 With which country do we associate haggis?

3 Of which country is Accra the capital?

4 Whose catchphrase was 'Who loves ya, baby'?

5 From which language do the words 'rabbi', 'amen' and 'kosher' originate?

6 What is the name of the famous French policeman played by Peter Sellers in the Pink Panther films?

7 In which year did the first Brook Advisory Clinic open to give birth control advice?

8 What is the name of the society that re-enacts historical scenes from the English Civil War?

9 Who first proposed the theory of relativity?

10 What is the nineteenth hole of a golf course?

ANSWERS

1. REM (Rapid Eye Movement) sleep. 2. Scotland. 3. Ghana. 4. 'Kojak'.
5. Hebrew. 6. 'Inspector Jacques Clousseau'. 7. 1964. 8. The Sealed Knot
Society. 9. Albert Einstein. 10. The bar of the clubhouse.

QUIZ 66

• •

1   With which country do we associate pizzas?

2   What is the raising agent in a cheese soufflé?

3   What is the name of the Danes, Norwegians and Swedes who raided Europe from the 8th to the 11th centuries?

4   Who wrote Four Quartets and The Waste Land?

5   In which year did J. Sainsbury open the first self-service store in Britain?

6   Who wrote the poems The Rime of the Ancient Mariner and Kubla Khan?

7   Who do the initials KFC stand for?

8   Who was the first Director-General of the BBC?

9   What is the name of the RAF jet aircraft aerobatics display team?

10 In which year was Lady Chatterley's Lover published?

ANSWERS

1. Italy. 2. Eggs. 3. Vikings. 4. T. S. Eliot. 5. 1950. 6. Samuel Taylor Coleridge.
7. Kentucky Fried Chicken. 8. John Reith, 1st Baron. 9. The Red Arrows.
10. 1960.

QUIZ 67

• •

1 What was the name of the yacht in which Sir Francis Chichester sailed around the world in 1966–67?

2 What is the stage name of Harry Roger Webb?

3 In radio, what do the initials CB stand for?

4 From which language do the words 'taffeta', 'bazaar' and 'caravan' originate?

5 Who wrote the novel Frankenstein?

6 Who was the 39th president of the USA?

7 What do the initials PVC stand for?

8 With which country do we associate sweet and sour dishes?

9 What do the initials RSI stand for?

10 Which canal links the Atlantic and Pacific Oceans?

ANSWERS

1. Gipsy Moth IV. 2. Cliff Richard. 3. Citizens' Band. 4. Persian. 5. Mary Shelley.
6. Jimmy Carter. 7. Polyvinyl chloride. 8. China. 9. Repetitive strain injury.
10. The Panama Canal.

QUIZ 68

• •

1. With which country do we associate moussaka?

2. 'Nation shall speak peace unto nation' is the motto of which British institution?

3. What was the name of the kind of art that was popular in the late 1960s and was marked by swirling patterns of vivid colours?

4. Who hosted the TV talent spotting show Opportunity Knocks?

5. Which philosopher wrote The Republic?

6. Where is the Monaco Grand Prix held?

7. What was the name of the US Air Force base near Newbury at which anti-nuclear protesters set up camp?

8. What was the name of the three BBC TV science fiction series broadcast in the 1950s?

9. According to the proverb, who cannot be choosers?

10. What do the initials FBI stand for?

ANSWERS

1. Greece. 2. The BBC. 3. Psychedelic. 4. Hughie Green. 5. Plato. 6. In the streets of Monte Carlo. 7. Greenham Common. 8. Quatermass. 9. Beggars. 10. Federal Bureau of Investigation.

QUIZ 69

1. According to legend, who was fiddling while Rome burned?

2. What do the initials PRO stand for?

3. The predictions of which 16th century French prophet were used by the Nazis in World War II?

4. With which country do we associate paella?

5. Nepotism is (a) criticism, (b) favouritism, or (c) authoritarianism?

6. Which Australian singer who moved to Britain in the 1950s is well known for playing the didgeridoo?

7. Which satirical magazine was first published in October 1961?

8. In which year was the Barbie doll first produced?

9. Who played Dr Kildare in the TV series of that name?

10. What was Windscale later known as?

ANSWERS

1. Nero. 2. Public Relations Officer. 3. Nostradamus. 4. Spain. 5. (b) favouritism. 6. Rolf Harris. 7. Private Eye. 8. 1959. 9. Richard Chamberlain. 10. Sellafield.

QUIZ 70

. . . .

1 In which year did the government launch its campaign 'Careless Talk Costs Lives'?

2 The slogan ' It's the real thing' was used to advertise what product?

3 In which chapter of the book of Exodus in the Bible are the Ten Commandments quoted?

4 What is the connection between an explanation of the origin of the universe and the major modernization, in 1986, of the London Stock Exchange?

5 How are you travelling if you do so as the crow flies?

6 What is the common name for the larynx?

7 Who created the character 'Biggles'?

8 What is the name of the practice of raising the price of a house after agreeing a price verbally with an intended buyer?

9 In which county is the River Medway?

10 Which famous military march was written by Major F. J. Ricketts?

ANSWERS

1. 1940. 2. Coca-Cola. 3. Chapter 20. 4. They are both called the Big Bang.
5. In a straight line. 6. Voice box. 7. Captain W. E. Johns. 8. Gazumping.
9. Kent. 10. 'Coloney Bogey'.

QUIZ 71

. . . .

1 Who said that his goal was thanks to 'the hand of God'?

2 Where is Traitors' Gate?

3 Which German village is famous for its Passion Play performed every ten years in thanksgiving for the end of the Black Death?

4 Which town is the capital of the Isle of Man?

5 What died on 29 August 1882?

6 Who wrote the play Cavalcade?

7 Which Scottish novelist and dramatist in his play Housemaster wrote: 'Funny peculiar, or funny ha-ha'?

8 St Francis de Sales is the patron saint of whom?

9 Which novelist created the characters 'Bertie Wooster' and 'Jeeves'?

10 If your surname is 'Murphy', what might your nickname be?

ANSWERS

1. Maradona. 2. The Tower of London. 3. Oberammergau. 4. Douglas.
5. English cricket, after the England cricket team's defeat by the Australians; the 'ashes' were taken to Australia. 6. Noël Coward. 7. Ian Hay (John Hay Beith). 8. Authors and journalists. 9. P. G. Wodehouse. 10. 'Spud'.

QUIZ 72

• •

1 Which English painter is known for his paintings of bleak industrial scenes with dark, matchsticklike figures?

2 Who, or what, is 'Ernie'?

3 What is the meaning of the expression 'lily livered': (a) cowardly, (b) brave or (c) white?

4 Osiris was a god of ancient Egypt. What was his domain?

5 What did 'Tonto' always call the 'Lone Ranger'?

6 Who was Sir Frank Brangwyn?

7 Who won the Five Nations Rugby Union Championship in 1997?

8 What does it signify when eight bells are sounded at sea?

9 The Jolly Roger is the traditional flag of what?

10 Westminster Abbey is over 166 metres long. True or false?

ANSWERS

1. L. S. Lowry. 2. The Electronic Random Number Indicator Equipment for drawing Premium Bonds. 3. (a) cowardly. 4. The underworld. 5. 'Kemo Sabe'.
6. Artist, illustrator and designer. 7. France. 8. The end of a watch of four hours. 9. Pirates. 10. True.

QUIZ 73

• •

1   According to the fairy story, who was the long-haired beauty who is locked in a tower by a witch?

2   What is euchre?

3   From which Shakespeare play does the phrase 'at one fell swoop' come?

4   St Agatha is the patron saint of whom?

5   Which song was popular during the Civil Rights Movement in the US and is sung by groups protesting against unfair treatment?

6   Which close relative of the onion has a similar, but more delicate flavour?

7   According to the nursery rhyme, where did 'Doctor Foster' go to?

8   To what did Buncombe, North Carolina, give its name?

9   From which language do the words 'dachshund', 'lager' and 'frankfurter' originate?

10 A penny farthing is a type of what?

ANSWERS

1. 'Rapùnzel'. 2. A card game. 3. Macbeth. 4. Nurses. 5. 'We Shall Overcome'.
6. The leek. 7. Gloucester. 8. Bunkum or nonsense. 9. German. 10. Bicycle.

QUIZ 74

. . . .

1 Who wrote Old Possum's Book of Practical Cats?

2 If your surname is Miller, what might your nickname be?

3 Who coined the expression 'one-upmanship'?

4 What does an epidemic become when it spreads across many countries?

5 What is the capital of Australia?

6 Which word, beginning with 'post', means 'published after the death of the composer or author?'

7 What is the connection between walking under a ladder and breaking a mirror?

8 What kind of food item comes from Bakewell?

9 Who coined the slogan, 'All animals are created equal but some are more equal than others'?

10 Which country is denoted by the prefix 'Luso-'?

ANSWERS

1. T. S. Eliot. 2. Dusty. 3. Stephen Potter. 4. A pandemic. 5. Canberra.
6. Posthumous. 7. Bad luck. 8. A tart. 9. George Orwell. 10. Portugal.

QUIZ 75

1 What is a chateaubriand?

2 If you suffered from theophobia, what would you fear?

3 Who wrote the poem I Wandered Lonely as a Cloud?

4 Who was the first 'Supermac'?

5 In which city is the Champs Élysées?

6 In which county is Stansted Airport?

7 According to the nursery rhyme, what was the queen eating in the parlour?

8 In a pack of cards, which way does the king of spades look, to his left or to his right?

9 What was the name of Agatha Christie's first detective novel?

10 What does 'kosher' mean?

ANSWERS

1. A thick, large fillet steak. 2. God. 3. William Wordsworth. 4. Harold Macmillan. 5. Paris. 6. Essex. 7. Bread and honey. 8. To his left. 9. The Mysterious Affair at Styles. 10. Fit to be eaten according to Jewish law.

QUIZ 76

1 Who wrote Watership Down?

2 Which musician was known as 'Flash Harry'?

3 Off which country's north-east coast is the Great Barrier Reef?

4 Who was Sir Malcolm Campbell?

5 What word is used to refer to both a woman's loose long-sleeved blouse and a kind of biscuit containing a layer of currants?

6 What is a group of geese called?

7 Of what two main ingredients does a Bloody Mary consist?

8 Who founded the National Viewers and Listeners Association?

9 'Boys and girls come out to play, the moon doth...' Finish the line from the nursery rhyme.

10 Who made the phrase, 'Clunk, Click – Every Trip' famous?

ANSWERS

1. Richard Adams. 2. Sir Malcolm Sargent. 3. Australia. 4. Land-speed and water-speed record holder. 5. Garibaldi. 6. A gaggle. 7. Vodka and tomato juice. 8. Mary Whitehouse. 9. '...shine as bright as day'. 10. Jimmy Savile.

QUIZ 77

• •

1 Which saint's feast day falls on 26 December?

2 What is a 'blockbuster'?

3 Whose last words were: 'Oh, I am so bored with it all'?

4 The fava, or Windsor bean, is better known as what?

5 Who wrote the Doctor Dolittle books?

6 Which European princess had children named Albert, Caroline and Stephanie?

7 From which language do the words 'brandy', 'coleslaw' and 'sloop' originate?

8 Who is the patron saint of sailors?

9 What team has Alex Ferguson been manager of since 1986?

10 Who was Honoré de Balzac?

ANSWERS

1. St Stephen. 2. A great success, as of a book, film or stage show. 3. Sir Winston Churchill. 4. The broad bean. 5. Hugh Lofting. 6. Princess Grace of Monaco. 7. Dutch. 8. St Cuthbert. 9. Manchester United. 10. French novelist.

QUIZ 78

. . . .

1 What is named after the Australian gardener Maria Ann Smith?

2 What is an agnostic?

3 In the nursery rhyme beginning 'cock a doodle doo', what had 'my dame' lost in the next line?

4 According to the 'language of flowers', what does the veronica signify?

5 Who was the captain of the England women's cricket team between 1966 and 1977?

6 Which anniversary does an iron or sugar-candy wedding celebrate?

7 In 1991, Anthony Hopkins won the Academy Award for Best Actor in which film?

8 Which is the holy city of Hindus?

9 Clark Kent is a reporter for which newspaper?

10 What is a dolma?

ANSWERS

1. Granny Smith apples. 2. Someone who believes that we cannot know whether God exists or not. 3. Her shoe. 4. Fidelity. 5. Rachel Heyhoe-Flint. 6. The sixth. 7. The Silence of the Lambs. 8. Varanasi (Benares). 9. Daily Planet. 10. A vine or cabbage leaf with savoury stuffing.

QUIZ 79

1 What does a couch potato do all the time?

2 What is a bruxelloise?

3 From which language do the words 'fascism', 'fiasco' and 'pizza' originate?

4 Who was the Beast of Bolsover?

5 What is the name of the Greek version of the Old Testament?

6 What is colcannon?

7 What is the name of the old English country dancing performed outdoors by men who wear special white clothes to which small bells are often fixed?

8 Who in the world would be called 'Digger'?

9 Who wrote Titus Groan and Gormenghast?

10 The goat represents which sign of the Zodiac?

ANSWERS

1. Watch television. 2. A French sauce for asparagus. 3. Italian. 4. Dennis Skinner. 5. The Septuagint. 6. An Irish dish of mashed potatoes and cabbage. 7. Morris dancing. 8. An Australian. 9. Mervyn Peake. 10. Capricorn.

QUIZ 80

• •

1 Who wrote Winnie the Pooh?

2 What is vermouth?

3 What is the name for a five line poem in which the first two and the last lines rhyme?

4 If you were a printer, how many points would make an inch?

5 In which country is the Taurus mountain range?

6 Until 1935, by what name was Iran known?

7 In the nursery rhyme, what could 'Jack Sprat's wife' not eat?

8 Who, or what, is the old Lady of Threadneedle Street?

9 What is the name of the fruit developed as a hybrid of the loganberry, blackberry and raspberry?

10 'Grapnel' and 'kedge' are types of what?

ANSWERS

1. A. A. Milne. 2. A wine-based drink flavoured with herbs. 3. A LIMERICK.
4. Twelve. 5. Turkey. 6. Persia. 7. No lean. 8. The Bank of England.
9. Boysenberry. 10. Anchor.

QUIZ 81

• •

1 What were Laurel and Hardy's first names?

2 What is a 'shemozzle'?

3 Which Welsh designer of fabrics in a floral Victorian style opened a chain of shops under her own name in the 1960s?

4 Which country was the home of 'Dracula'?

5 From which language do the words 'marmalade' and 'molasses' originate?

6 In which sport does it matter if you get an 'LBW'?

7 In the story, who eats 'Little Red Ridinghood's Grandmother'?

8 What's the connection between baloney and polony?

9 According to the Bible, what were the names of the sons of Adam and Eve?

10 Scorpions are immune to their own poison. True or false?

ANSWERS

1. Stan and Oliver. 2. A mess, row or rumpus. 3. Laura Ashley.
4. Transylvania. 5. Portuguese. 6. Cricket (Leg Before Wicket). 7. A wolf.
8. From the Bologna sausage: the first means 'rubbish, nonsense', and the second is the sausage (US version). 9. Cain and Abel. 10. False.

QUIZ 82

• •

1   Who do the initials SAS stand for?

2   What are crocodile tears?

3   From which language do the words 'bamboo', 'sago' and 'batik' originate?

4   What do the initials R & R stand for?

5   For what was the slogan 'All human life is there' used to advertise?

6   With which country do we associate poppadoms and chapattis?

7   St Peter is the patron saint of whom?

8   A Bramley is what kind of fruit?

9   What is fascism?

10 Which is Scotland's largest lake?

ANSWERS

1. Special Air Service. 2. False tears. 3. Malay. 4. Rest (or relaxation) and recreation. 5. News of the World. 6. India. 7. Fishermen. 8. Apple.
9. A system of government which has only one political party headed by a dictator. 10. Loch Lomond.

QUIZ 83

- -

1　In which country is the Isle of Capri?

2　Who wrote The Book of Household Management?

3　What phrase, which originated in Punch magazine, is used to refer to something that is good in parts?

4　What is the name given to the beam placed above a window or door?

5　In which year was John Lennon shot?

6　Which character in the Bible asked 'What is truth?'

7　According to the New Testament, which Roman governor condemned Jesus to death?

8　Who wrote the Pollyanna novels?

9　With which sport is Henry Cooper associated?

10　Who succeeded Richard Nixon as US president in 1974?

ANSWERS

1. Italy. 2. Mrs (Isabella) Beeton. 3. Like a curate's egg. 4. Lintel. 5. 1980.
6. Pontius Pilate. 7. Gustav Holst. 8. Eleanor H. Porter. 9. Boxing.
10. Gerald Ford.

QUIZ 84

• •

1 From which country does Emmenthal cheese come?

2 Proverbially, out of what should we not make a mountain?

3 In the Bible, which donkey was given the power of speech?

4 What is the eighth letter of the Greek alphabet?

5 From which animal does chèvre come?

6 Which 'everyday story of country folk' celebrated 40 years of broadcasting in 1990?

7 Who was Jesus?

8 Who designed the 'bouncing bombs' used to break up dams during World War II?

9 What was the occupation of Sir Jacob Epstein?

10 Whose Symphony No.9 is 'from the New World'?

ANSWERS

1. Switzerland. 2. A molehill. 3. Balaam's donkey. 4. Theta. 5. Goat.
6. The Archers. 7. Christians believe he was the Son of God, and part of the
Trinity. 8. Barnes Wallis. 9. Sculptor. 10. Dvorak.

QUIZ 85

• •

1 What was Uri Geller famous for?

2 What is Thomas Bewick famous for?

3 Who coined the phrase 'God is dead'?

4 Who wrote the words of the hymn 'Amazing Grace'?

5 How long did rationing last during and after World War II?

6 Which German historian, in 1973, designed a modified map projection, aiming to show countries more accurately according to their true size?

7 What word, beginning with 'ante-', means 'going before, in time'?

8 Which country joined the European Union in 1981?

9 What is an ampersand?

10 In which year did Bobby and Jack Charlton retire from football?

ANSWERS

1. Bending spoons. 2. Engravings in wood and metal. 3. Nietzsche.
4. John Newton. 5. Fourteen and a half years. 6. Arno Peters. 7. Antecedent.
8. Greece. 9. The symbol & meaning 'and'. 10. 1973.

QUIZ 86

· ·

1 Which philosophy was founded by L. Ron Hubbard?

2 What was Oliver Hardy's catchphrase?

3 'Gazza' is the nickname for who?

4 In computer language, what is 'spam'?

5 What country is called Blighty?

6 What is the name of the US TV programme for young children that teaches numbers and letters, and whose characters include 'Big Bird' and the 'Cookie Monster'?

7 What does 'schmaltz' mean?

8 In politics who was nicknamed 'The Iron Lady'?

9 How much was a pennyweight?

10 Who has been leader of the PLO since 1969?

ANSWERS

1. Scientology. 2.'Here's another fine mess you've gotten me into'. 3. Paul Gascoigne. 4. Unwanted e-mail messages. 5. England. 6. Sesame Street. 7. Sickly sweet, sentimental. 8. Margaret Thatcher. 9. Twenty-four grains. 10. Yasser Arafat.

QUIZ 87

• •

1 What is a brioche?

2 What do the initials SEATO stand for?

3 Who was known as the Lady of the Lamp?

4 Who directed the films Mr Smith Goes to Washington and It's a Wonderful Life?

5 The word 'recondite' means (a) difficult to understand, (b) talkative, or (c) valuable?

6 According to the nursery rhyme, what did the cow jump over?

7 Which day is the Jewish sabbath?

8 In which county is Lizard Point, the southernmost point in the British Isles?

9 What is stroganoff?

10 In which country is Vesuvius?

ANSWERS

1. A kind of soft roll or loaf. 2. South East Asia Treaty Organization.
3. Florence Nightingale. 4. Frank Capra. 5. (a) difficult to understand.
6. The Moon. 7. Saturday. 8. Cornwall. 9. Thinly-cut meat, onions and mushrooms in a sour cream sauce. 10. Italy.

QUIZ 88

1. 'Rapacity' means (a) greed, (b) haste or (c) severity?

2. Who shot Lee Harvey Oswald?

3. Which lesbian actor came out and saw her TV ratings fall dramatically?

4. Which BBC news correspondent became an MP at the general election in 1997?

5. What is an ostrich reputed to do when being pursued?

6. Who is the one-legged sailor with a parrot on his shoulder that is the main character in Treasure Island?

7. St Sebastian is the patron saint of whom?

8. Who wrote The Wind in the Willows?

9. The fish represent which sign of the Zodiac?

10. In which country is the Simpson Desert?

ANSWERS

1. (a) greed. 2. Jack Ruby. 3. Ellen DeGeneres. 4. Martin Bell. 5. Bury its head in the sand. 6. 'Long John Silver'. 7. Athletes. 8. Kenneth Grahame. 9. Pisces. 10. Australia.

QUIZ 89

1 What was the name of the fat and greedy schoolboy created by Frank Richards?

2 What do the initials NIMBY stand for?

3 What does the Russian word 'glasnost' mean?

4 What do the initials EFTPOS stand for?

5 The Oder-Neisse line marked the frontier between which two countries after World War II?

6 On which island (to which he had been exiled) did John write the book of Revelation?

7 Who is Allah?

8 Who wrote the words, 'If I should die, think only this of me: That there's some corner of a foreign field that is forever England'?

9 Who wrote 'Auld Lang Syne' and 'Tam O'Shanter'?

10 Who, according to the nursery rhyme, killed 'Cock Robin'?

ANSWERS

1. 'Billy Bunter'. 2. Not in my back yard. 3. Openness. 4. Electronic funds transfer at point of sale. 5. Germany and Poland. 6. Patmos. 7. According to the Muslims, the Supreme Being, or God. 8. Rupert Brooke. 9. Robert Burns. 10. 'The Sparrow'.

QUIZ 90

• •

1 In which book come the words 'It is a far, far better thing that I do, than I have ever done; it is a far, far better rest that I go to, than I have ever known'?

2 Who was the first woman to read the main evening news on BBC TV?

3 What was the nickname of Louis Armstrong?

4 From which language do the words 'bungalow', 'chintz' and 'bangle' originate?

5 Who starred in the film Rebel Without A Cause?

6 Who wrote Westward Ho!?

7 If your surname is 'Martin', what might your nickname be?

8 What do the initials MCP stand for?

9 A culverin is (a) a cannon, (b) a gutter or (c) a unit of coinage?

10 In which film did 'George Dixon' first appear?

ANSWERS

1. A Tale of Two Cities. 2. Angela Rippon. 3. Satchmo. 4. Hindi. 5. James Dean. 6. Charles Kingsley. 7. Pincher. 8. Male chauvinist pig. 9. (a) a cannon. 10. The Blue Lamp.

QUIZ 91

● ●

1. From which language do the words 'robot', 'pistol' and 'howitzer' originate?

2. Which anniversary does a crystal wedding celebrate?

3. Which novel set in Yorkshire features 'Catherine Earnshaw' and 'Heathcliff'?

4. What does 'circa' or 'c.' in connection with dates mean?

5. A kohlrabi is a cross between which two vegetables?

6. To which American film producer is 'in two words: im-possible' attributed?

7. What is the name of the stretch of water between Denmark and Sweden?

8. In which country is the River Fraser?

9. What anniversary does a wooden wedding celebrate?

10. Who was 'the marmalade cat'?

ANSWERS

1. Czech. 2. The fifteenth. 3. Wuthering Heights. 4. About or around.
5. A cabbage and a turnip. 6. Samuel Goldwyn. 7. Kattegat. 8. Canada.
9. The fifth. 10. 'Orlando'.

QUIZ 92

• •

1 When was the Samaritans founded?

2 Water is also known as whose 'ale'?

3 Who was 'Lady Penelope's' chauffeur?

4 Of what group does one find a posse?

5 According to Greek myth what was Nemesis the goddess of?

6 Who is the patron saint of workers?

7 Who wrote The Lord of the Rings?

8 In 'A Christmas Carol' what is Scrooge's first name?

9 What common sight in urban town centres derives its name from the Minister of Transport for 1934 to 1937?

10 What are gnocchi?

ANSWERS

1. 1953. 2. Adam. 3. 'Parker'. 4. Cowboys, constables, police. 5. Retribution and vengeance. 6. St Joseph. 7. J. R. R. Tolkein. 8. Ebenezer. 9. Belisha beacon, named after 1st Baron Leslie Hore-Belisha. 10. Italian savoury dumplings.

QUIZ 93

• •

1 From which language do the words 'tsar', 'steppe' and 'vodka' originate?

2 What is an éclair?

3 What does the prefix 'neo' mean?

4 Who is the reigning monarch of Japan?

5 What is Modulator and Demodulator more commonly called?

6 The twins represent which sign of the Zodiac?

7 In which ocean is the island of Mauritius?

8 Whose statue stands in front of Wesley's Chapel in City Road, London?

9 In the Bible, what virtue was Job famous for?

10 Who said, 'Father, I cannot tell a lie'?

ANSWERS

1. Russian. 2. A long, light pastry with custard or cream filling and chocolate sauce. 3. New or revived. 4. Emperor Akihito. 5. A modem. 6. Gemini. 7. The Indian Ocean. 8. John Wesley. 9. His patience. 10. George Washington.

QUIZ 94

. . . .

1 Who played 'The Prisoner' in the TV series of that name?

2 The 'jolly swagman' went 'Waltzing Matilda'. What was a matilda?

3 Which Czech-born newspaper owner and businessman died suddenly, falling into the water from his boat?

4 How did teddy bears receive their name?

5 What is the name of the founding prophet of the Islamic faith?

6 In wartime, what was a WAAF?

7 What does the prefix 'cardio-' mean?

8 Which architect designed Waterloo Bridge and the Anglican Cathedral in Liverpool?

9 Who, in 1976, opened her first Body Shop?

10 What kind of food is baklava?

ANSWERS

1. Patrick McGoohan. 2. The swagman's roll containing his blanket.
3. Robert Maxwell. 4. They were named after the American president,
Theodore 'Teddy' Roosevelt. 5. Mohammed. 6. A member of the Women's
Auxiliary Air Force. 7. To do with the heart. 8. Sir Giles Gilbert Scott. 9. Anita
Roddick. 10. Pastry filled with nuts and honey.

QUIZ 95

. . . .

1   Who wrote Hancock's Half Hour?

2   What does 'bespoke' mean (a) to do with a bicycle, (b) made-to-measure or (c) committed?

3   What is the correct name of the Christian denomination commonly referred to as the 'Quakers'?

4   What is a quiche?

5   What sort of creature is a drongo?

6   In Cockney rhyming slang, what is meant by 'plates of meat'?

7   What does the prefix 'kilo' mean?

8   Mercury is another name for the messenger of the gods, Hermes. True or false?

9   Who played 'Meg Richardson' in the TV soap Crossroads?

10 Which anniversary does a golden wedding celebrate?

ANSWERS

1. Ray Galton and Alan Simpson. 2. (b) made-to-measure. 3. The Religious Society of Friends. 4. A shell of unsweetened pastry which can hold a savoury filling. 5. A bird. 6. Feet. 7. Thousand. 8. True. 9. Noele Gordon. 10. The fiftieth.

QUIZ 96

. . . .

1 In which modern-day country did the ancient city of Troy lie?

2 What is a 'Walter Mitty'?

3 From which language do the words 'fjord', 'floe' and 'slalom' originate?

4 In which city, apart from London, would you find Soho?

5 What is Neil Armstrong famous for?

6 What is cribbage?

7 Alpha, epsilon and lambda are all what?

8 Which musical play featured the song 'Climb Ev'ry Mountain'?

9 In which year was the Berlin Wall destroyed?

10 Campanology is the art of what?

ANSWERS

1. Turkey. 2. A day-dreaming fantasist. 3. Norwegian. 4. Birmingham.
5. Being the first man to walk on the Moon. 6. A card game. 7. Letters in
the Greek alphabet. 8. The Sound of Music. 9. 1989. 10. Ringing bells.

QUIZ 101

. . . .

1 Who first said, 'A week is a long time in politics'?

2 In which city is the Heriot-Watt university?

3 Little Moreton Hall is an example of what kind of house?

4 Where can the Venus de Milo be seen?

5 In which German city does the Oktoberfest take place?

6 What did Mrs Mary Baker Eddy found?

7 Mars was the Roman god of what?

8 What are profiteroles?

9 Which poet wrote The Divine Comedy?

10 St Isidore is the patron saint of whom?

ANSWERS

1. Harold Wilson. 2. Edinburgh. 3. Timber frame. 4. The Louvre, Paris.
5. Munich. 6. Christian Science. 7. War. 8. Small puffs of choux pastry, filled with cream and covered in chocolate sauce. 9. Dante. 10. Farmers.

QUIZ 102

. . . .

1 What kind of creature is an impala?

2 Who is the patron saint of travellers?

3 How, in art, is the god Janus depicted?

4 What is a madeleine?

5 From which language do the words 'cobalt', 'nickel' and 'quartz' originate?

6 What do the initials SAS stand for?

7 On which river does the border town of Berwick stand?

8 What famous landmark stands on the site of Tyburn Tree in London?

9 Where in Britain is 'Spaghetti Junction'?

10 Who chaired 'Juke Box Jury'?

ANSWERS

1. An antelope. 2. St Christopher. 3. With two heads each facing opposite ways. 4. A small, shell-shaped sponge cake. 5. German. 6. Special Air Service. 7. Tweed. 8. Marble Arch. 9. Gravelly Hill motorway interchange, Birmingham. 10. David Jacobs.

QUIZ 103

1 In financial terms, what do the initials IMF stand for?

2 Which anniversary does a silver wedding celebrate?

3 Where did troglodytes live?

4 Wednesday is named after 'Woden', the German god of war. True or false?

5 With which country do we associate flamenco dancing?

6 What Italian artist was also an architect, philosopher, poet, composer, sculptor and mathematician?

7 What shop traditionally had a pole painted in red and white stripes outside?

8 Where did the Flintstones live?

9 Who is the patron saint of television?

10 Who in the world would be called a Canuck?

ANSWERS

1. International Monetary Fund. 2. The twenty-fifth. 3. In a cave. 4. True.
5. Spain. 6. Leonardo da Vinci. 7. A barber's. 8. Bedrock. 9. St Clare.
10. A Canadian.

QUIZ 104

1 Which knighted author wrote a famous novel about Kenilworth in Warwickshire?

2 Why were the first London policemen called 'peelers'?

3 Proverbially, what is just 'skin deep'?

4 What is Cumberland sauce?

5 What do flags flying at half mast indicate?

6 What were, or are, the Gnomes of Zurich?

7 From the Bible what name do we give to the social outcast who takes care of a man who had been mugged and beaten and whose plight had been ignored by others?

8 A magnum is a measure of wine equivalent to how many bottles?

9 What is the name of the local public house in Coronation Street?

10 What did George Cruikshank do?

ANSWERS

1. Sir Walter Scott. 2. They were first organized by Sir Robert Peel.
3. Beauty. 4. A redcurrant sauce with lemons, oranges, and port wine.
5. A sign of mourning or distress. 6. Swiss bankers and financiers.
7. Good Samaritan. 8. Two. 9. 'The Rovers Return'. 10. He was a caricaturist and illustrator of books.

QUIZ 105

• •

1 What is a 'Lent lily' better known as?

2 According to the 'language of flowers', what does the peony signify?

3 Which city is famous for its Temple of Artemis?

4 'Rule by the people as a whole' is called what?

5 What is the square root of nine?

6 Which word, beginning with 'ante-', means 'to date, before true time'?

7 When was the 'Glorious First of June'?

8 Who was the Boston Strangler?

9 Which Jewish festival is also known as the 'Feast of Lights'?

10 What is the name of the young girl who plays a leading part in Peter Pan?

ANSWERS

1. Daffodil. 2. Shame or bashfulness. 3. Ephesus. 4. Democracy. 5. Three. 6. Antedate. 7. 1 June 1794, the date of the British naval victory over the French. 8. Albert de Salvo. 9. Chanukah. 10. Wendy.

QUIZ 106

. . . .

1 What are the three Rs?

2 Samson, a judge of Israel, possessed what great gift?

3 Of which country is Baghdad the capital?

4 Who was the author of the 'Noddy' books?

5 What number, according to The Hitch Hiker's Guide to the Galaxy, is the answer to the ultimate question of life, the universe and everything?

6 Name two well known plays by Terence Rattigan.

7 Where were 'ten green bottles'?

8 Poseidon is another name for Neptune. True or false?

9 Whose favourite expression was 'Exterminate! Exterminate!'

10 What is the third book of the Bible?

ANSWERS

1. Reading, writing and arithmetic. 2. Enormous strength. 3. Iraq. 4. Enid Blyton. 5. 42. 6. Flare Path, French Without Tears, While the Sun Shines, The Winslow Boy. 7. Standing on the wall. 8. True. 9. The 'Daleks'. 10. Leviticus.

QUIZ 107

. . . .

1 In which poem do 'slithy toves' originate?

2 The 'Abominable Snowman' is also known as?

3 Which proverb do we use to say that we should not judge a thing by its attractive golden appearance?

4 The water carrier represents which sign of the Zodiac?

5 In which year was the first Benson & Hedges Cup held?

6 What is the name given to the informal version of French that contains a large number of English words?

7 In A Christmas Carol by Charles Dickens, who does Scrooge receive a visit from?

8 What is chilli con carne?

9 According to the Bible, who refused to accept the truth of the resurrected Christ until he had actually seen and touched Christ's body for himself?

10 In the year 1752, what date followed 2 September?

ANSWERS

1. Jabberwocky by Lewis Carroll. 2. The Yeti. 3. All that glitters is not gold.
4. Aquarius. 5. 1972. 6. Franglais. 7. 'The ghost of Marley'. 8. Minced meat, beans and chillis. 9. Thomas. 10. 14 September. The calendar had changed and eleven days were omitted.

QUIZ 108

• •

1 In which English county is the holiday resort of Morecambe?

2 Who was Sheridan Morley's father?

3 What is the name of the Dutch graphic artist who is well known for his drawings that distort perspective and deceive the eye?

4 What is abalone?

5 Which pocket-sized monthly magazine was first published in America in 1922?

6 What is the literal meaning of the word 'karaoke'?

7 Who wrote the novel Catch 22?

8 What does ROM stand for in computing?

9 Proverbially, where does charity begin?

10 Which theatre in London was originally called the Waldorf?

ANSWERS

1. Lancashire. 2. Robert Morley. 3. M. C. Escher. 4. A mollusc, like the sea snail, with a flat, oval shell. 5. Reader's Digest. 6. Empty orchestra. 7. Joseph Heller. 8. Read Only Memory. 9. At home. 10. The Strand.

QUIZ 109

1 Who wrote the Thomas the Tank Engine stories?

2 What instrument did Niccolo Paganini play?

3 According to the Bible, what was the name of the paradise created for Adam and Eve?

4 St Michael was the patron saint of whom?

5 In American slang, what is a shamus?

6 What was a 'doughboy'?

7 In biology, what is the term given to the ability of an organism to replace one of its parts if it is lost?

8 What does 'in the buff' mean?

9 What do the initials UAE stand for?

10 Which daily newspaper was first published on 7 October 1986?

ANSWERS

1. Rev W. Audrey. 2. The violin. 3. The Garden of Eden. 4. Soldiers. 5. A police officer or private detective. 6. An American soldier. 7. Regeneration. 8. Naked. 9. United Arab Emirates. 10. The Independent.

QUIZ 110

• •

1 Which book of the Bible begins 'In the beginning was the Word'?

2 If your birthday was 5 April, what star sign would you be?

3 Proverbially, what is in the eye of the beholder?

4 What is meant by 'Dutch courage'?

5 Who wrote the play Happy Days in 1961?

6 What is a Bath bun?

7 In which English county is the holiday resort of Bournemouth?

8 What does the name of the city Philadelphia mean?

9 In Greek mythology, who was condemned to hold up the heavens on his shoulders for his lifetime?

10 What was the name of the early Australian coach and mail company?

ANSWERS

1. The Gospel of John. 2. Aries. 3. Beauty. 4. Courage with the aid of strong liquor. 5. Samuel Beckett. 6. A rich, rather sweet, bun. 7. Dorset. 8. City of brotherly love. 9. Atlas. 10. Cobb and Co.

QUIZ 111

• •

1   Who plays 'Mr Bean' in the comedy series of that name?

2   What is a sorbet?

3   In Gulliver's Travels, 'Gulliver's' second set of adventures takes place where?

4   What did American Express introduce in 1891?

5   Who wrote the drama Hedda Gabler?

6   The Bull represents which sign of the Zodiac?

7   Which was the last battle fought on British soil?

8   Name the Beatles' manager who died in 1967.

9   According to the Bible, where was a tower built to reach to the heavens?

10 Which country did 'Paddington Bear' come from?

ANSWERS

1. Rowan Atkinson. 2. A water ice. 3. Brobdingnag. 4. Travellers' cheques.
5. Henrik Ibsen. 6. Taurus. 7. Culloden. 8. Brian Epstein. 9. Babel. 10. Peru.

QUIZ 112

. . . .

1 Who said 'I am just going outside, and may be some time'?

2 Who in the world would be called 'Taffy'?

3 What was the popular name of the Thoughts of Chairman Mao?

4 Which word, beginning with 'post-', means 'those coming after'?

5 Who wrote The Lion, the Witch and the Wardrobe?

6 According to the book of Genesis, what did God set in the sky as a promise that he would never again destroy the world through a flood?

7 What is the singular of 'dice'?

8 What shade of colour is vermilion?

9 Who sponsors the British Telecom speaking clock?

10 What is the slogan on the World War I poster that featured Lord Kitchener's face and pointing hand?

ANSWERS

1. Captain Lawrence Oates, English Antarctic explorer. 2. A Welshman.
3. The Little Red Book. 4. Posterity. 5. C. S. Lewis. 6. A rainbow. 7. Die.
8. Bright red. 9. Accurist. 10. 'Your Country Needs You'.

QUIZ 113

. . . .

1 Who is 'Old Nick'?

2 What year was the Battle of Britain?

3 Köchel numbers refer to the works of which composer?

4 Which artist was renowned for his paintings of horses?

5 What do the initials DC stand for after 'Washington'?

6 How many farthings were there in half a crown?

7 Where in Britain would you find our oldest surviving clock?

8 In Roman mythology who was the messenger of the gods?

9 In which land did Gulliver's Travels take place?

10 What is a four-leaf clover supposed to be a sign of?

ANSWERS

1. The Devil. 2. 1940. 3. Mozart. 4. George Stubbs. 5. District of Columbia.
6. 120. 7. Salisbury Cathedral, whose clock dates from 1386. 8. Mercury.
9. Lilliput. 10. Good luck.

QUIZ 114

. . . .

1 Which mountain is Europe's highest?

2 Who in the world would be called a 'Jock'?

3 Who wrote the 'William' books?

4 A stitch in time will save how many?

5 In which year was John F. Kennedy assassinated?

6 How many is a baker's dozen?

7 What is a façade?

8 Which English artist gave his name to devices or contraptions that are absurdly complex in design?

9 Where is Britain's unknown soldier buried?

10 In which Scottish village was the TV series Dr Finlay's Casebook based?

ANSWERS

1. Elbrus. 2. A Scotsman. 3. Richmal Crompton. 4. Nine. 5. 1963. 6. 13.
7. The front of a building. 8. (William) Heath Robinson. 9. Westminster Abbey. 10. Tannochbrae.

QUIZ 115

1 Who launched his Virgin Atlantic airline in 1984?

2 The American cartoonist Chester Gould conceived which character?

3 Who left The Big Breakfast Show to concentrate on Don't Forget Your Toothbrush?

4 What does AWOL stand for?

5 Who wrote the Barchester novels?

6 In which century was tea first brought to England?

7 What is Albert sauce?

8 From which language do the words 'duet', 'piano' and 'soprano' originate?

9 What is the size of A4 paper?

10 Which character is the exploited clerk to 'Scrooge' in A Christmas Carol by Charles Dickens?

ANSWERS

1. Richard Branson. 2. Dick Tracy. 3. Chris Evans. 4. Absent Without Leave.
5. Anthony Trollope. 6. 17th century. 7. A sauce made with cream, butter,
horseradish, mustard and vinegar. 8. Italian. 9. 210 x 297 millimetres.
10. 'Bob Cratchit'.

QUIZ 116

- -

1 Who launched London Weekend Television's The South Bank Show in 1978?

2 In ancient times, what was King Midas's big problem?

3 Which character was also a civilian bank manager in Dad's Army?

4 Where is the Golden Gate?

5 What was the name of the American statesman who was the first to sign the Declaration of Independence and whose name has come to mean 'a signature'?

6 In which year were yellow and red cards introduced for misdemeanours in the English football league?

7 What is Bezique?

8 When was the single European currency, the euro, introduced?

9 If a foreign car displayed the letters RO, what would its country of origin be?

10 Name the capital of Iceland.

ANSWERS

1. Melvyn Bragg. 2. Everything he touched turned to gold. 3. 'Captain Mainwaring'. 4. The entrance to the bay of San Francisco. 5. John Hancock. 6. 1976. 7. A card game which originated in France. 8. 1 January 1999. 9. Romania. 10. Reykjavik.

QUIZ 117

. . . .

1 Who wrote a famous biography of Dr Johnson?

2 Which anniversary does a bronze or electrical appliance wedding celebrate?

3 Who wrote the 'Tintin' picture stories?

4 Which word, beginning with 'post-', means 'after dinner'?

5 Who played 'Sir Charles' in The Pink Panther?

6 In which British city would you find a lake called the Serpentine?

7 What did Alexander of Macedon and Alfred, King of England, have in common?

8 According to tradition, how many lives does a cat have?

9 What was nicknamed 'The Thunderer'?

10 Who wrote the children's novel Emil and the Detectives?

ANSWERS

1. James Boswell. 2. The eighth. 3. G. R. Hergé. 4. Postprandial. 5. David Niven. 6. London. 7. They were both known by the title 'The Great'. 8. Nine. 9. The Times newspaper. 10. Eric Kästner.

QUIZ 118

• •

1 What is the collective noun for a group of lions?

2 What city lies at the northernpost point of the River Danube?

3 What part did Kenneth More play in the film Genevieve?

4 Who was George Cadbury?

5 Who wrote the Waverley novels?

6 What is the name of the pessimistic donkey in the Winnie the Pooh stories?

7 In what place do Muslim people worship?

8 Who wrote the novel The Prime of Miss Jean Brodie?

9 What did the 'Owl and the Pussycat' go to sea in?

10 What was the profession of Lancelot (or 'Capability') Brown?

ANSWERS

1. A pride. 2. Regensburg. 3. 'Ambrose Claverhouse'. 4. A businessman and philanthropist from the famous chocolate firm. 5. Sir Walter Scott. 6. 'Eeyore'. 7. A mosque. 8. Muriel Spark. 9. A beautiful pea green boat. 10. Landscape gardener.

QUIZ 119

• •

1   What is the collective noun for a group of rhinoceros?

2   If something is held 'in camera', what does it mean?

3   Who directed the 1992 film Hook?

4   Sir William Alexander Smith founded what boys' organization?

5   Which sign of the Zodiac is represented by a pair of scales?

6   What proverb, originating from blacksmiths, means that we should not try to do too much at once?

7   How does the Archbishop of Canterbury sign himself?

8   What is the SI unit of electric current?

9   Who, in ancient times, were Shem, Ham and Japheth?

10 From which language does the word 'ombudsman' come?

ANSWERS

1. A crash. 2. In secret, with the public as a whole excluded. 3. Steven Spielberg. 4. The Boys' Brigade. 5. Libra. 6. Don't have too many irons in the fire. 7. His name, followed by Cantuar. 8. Ampere. 9. The sons of Noah. 10. Swedish.

QUIZ 120

• •

1   What is the collective noun for a group of crows?

2   Friday is named after 'Frigga', the German goddess of married love. True or false?

3   Who played 'Mrs Potts' in Disney's Beauty and the Beast?

4   What kind of food comes from Kendal?

5   When was decimal currency introduced in Britain?

6   Of which country is Berne the capital?

7   Which politician is known as 'Tarzan'?

8   From which play by Shakespeare does the expression 'Brave New World' come?

9   In which year was legionnaire's disease first described?

10 Who wrote The Tale of Peter Rabbit?

ANSWERS

1. A murder. 2. True. 3. Angela Lansbury. 4. A mint cake. 5. 1971. 6. Switzerland. 7. Michael Heseltine. 8. The Tempest. 9. 1976. 10. Beatrix Potter.

QUIZ 121

• •

1 Who are listed in the reference book Crockford's?

2 What was the occupation of 'Lovely Rita'?

3 What is the surname of the writer whose first names were William Makepeace?

4 Who, in a music-hall song, went to Crewe in mistake for Birmingham?

5 Which vegetable is traditionally hollowed out and used as a lantern at Hallowe'en?

6 What kind of fruit is a seville?

7 What is the Army equivalent of an Air Chief Marshal?

8 Who was the captain of HMS Bounty, in which the seamen and petty officers mutinied?

9 To which part of the USA does Dixieland refer to?

10 What is the code number for 'James Bond'?

ANSWERS

1. The clergy of the Church of England. 2. She was a traffic warden.
3. Thackeray. 4. Marie Lloyd. 5. A pumpkin. 6. Orange. 7. General. 8. William Bligh. 9. The southern states. 10. 007.

QUIZ 122

. . . .

1 What does cack-handed mean?

2 There are several sections of an orchestra: woodwind, percussion and strings are three, what is the fourth?

3 If you were 'in the altogether', what would you be?

4 Monapia was the ancient name for which island?

5 In cockney rhyming slang, what does 'pen and ink' mean?

6 What line follows, 'And did those feet in ancient time'?

7 Stories about 'Lord Snooty' and his pals appeared in which publication?

8 Piccadilly Railway station is in which city?

9 Vitamin D helps bone formation and keeps teeth healthy. True or false?

10 Who wrote The Adventures of Huckleberry Finn?

ANSWERS

1. Originally left-handed, but later clumsy. 2. Brass. 3. Naked. 4. The Isle of Man. 5. Stink. 6. 'Walk upon England's mountains green'. 7. The Beano. 8. Manchester. 9. True. 10. Mark Twain.

QUIZ 123

· ·

1 Victoria railway stations can be found in three cities in the world. Two of them are London and Bombay. Where is the other?

2 A yegg is: (a) an American safe-breaker, (b) a young Scottish calf or (c) a kind of hiccup?

3 The novel Rebeccca was written by whom?

4 In a pack of cards, the queen of Clubs looks to her left. True or false?

5 What is the language spoken in Catalonia, Spain?

6 What does an astronomer study?

7 A diplomatic envoy who represents his own head of state in a foreign country is known as a what?

8 What was the title of David Niven's biographical book?

9 An American soldier would go to the PX or post exchange, where would an English soldier go?

10 Who is the female 'James Bond' created by Peter O'Donnell?

ANSWERS

1. Manchester. 2. (a) an American safe breaker. 3. Daphne du Maurier.
4. True. 5. Catalan. 6. The stars. 7. An ambassador. 8. The Moon's a Balloon.
9. The NAAFI. 10. 'Modesty Blaise'.

QUIZ 124

. . . .

1 What is now the official name of the former Cambodia?

2 Which anniversary does a copper or pottery wedding celebrate?

3 A numismatist studies what two things?

4 Dublin stands on which river?

5 If Bill Brewer, Jan Stewer and Peter Gurney were the first three going somewhere, where would that be?

6 The Little Mermaid in Copenhagen is a memorial to whom?

7 What is the male version of the equine term 'dam'?

8 'Be prepared' is the motto of which group of people?

9 Istanbul is the modern name for which ancient city?

10 What was the nickname of ex-US president Richard Nixon?

ANSWERS

1. Kampuchea. 2. The ninth. 3. Coins and medals. 4. The River Liffey.
5. Widdicombe Fair. 6. Hans Christian Andersen. 7. Sire. 8. The Scouts.
9. Byzantium. 10. 'Tricky Dicky'.

QUIZ 125

• •

1 Where is Traitors' Gate?

2 St Matthew is the patron saint of whom?

3 In a pack of cards, which way does the King of Hearts look; to his left, or to his right?

4 What is a Peach Melba?

5 What is sauce lyonnaise?

6 What is taramasalata?

7 What nationality was Brother Jonathan?

8 What is known as the 'devil's bedpost'?

9 What are croutons?

10 What was the name of the early Australian coach and mail company?

ANSWERS

1. The Tower of London. 2. Accountants and bankers. 3. To his right. 4. Peach halves with ice-cream and raspberry sauce. 5. A sauce with white wine and onions. 6. A Greek 'dip' dish of smoked-fish or roe paste with olive oil, etc. 7. An American. 8. The four of clubs playing-card. 9. Small pieces of toast fried in butter. 10. Cobb and Co.

QUIZ 126

• •

1   Before decimalisation, our coinage used the letters £, s and d. What did they mean?

2   Which word beginning with ante- means 'before marriage'?

3   Who is the patron saint of teachers?

4   Which anniversary does a pearl wedding celebrate?

5   What, in medieval times, was a groat?

6   What is ravioli?

7   Who was George Cadbury?

8   Who, in ancient times, were Shem, Ham and Japheth?

9   Who, or what, is the Old Lady of Threadneedle Street?

10   In what groups does one find a squadron?

ANSWERS

1. The '£' sign is the Latin letter L for libra, pound. The 's' is for soldi, shillings, and 'd' for denarius, penny. 2. Antenuptial. 3. St Gregory. 4. The thirtieth. 5. Any thick, silver coin. 6. Small pasta cases with a savoury filling. 7 . A businessman and philanthropist from the famous chocolate firm. 8. The sons of Noah. 9. The Bank of England. 10. Aircraft, ships, soldiers.

QUIZ 127

1 Who wrote the play Cavalcade?

2 What is a rollmop?

3 According to the 'language of flowers', what does the asphodel signify?

4 Which anniversary does a sapphire wedding celebrate?

5 St David is the patron saint of what?

6 What is the Purple Heart?

7 What is hock?

8 Who, with his wife, was expelled from the Garden of Eden?

9 Rice paper isn't made from rice. What is it made from?

10 What is meant by 'Dutch courage'?

ANSWERS

1. Noël Coward. 2. A herring fillet rolled up with onion and pickled.
3. My regret follows you to the grave. 4. The forty-fifth. 5. Wales.
6. An American decoration awarded to soldiers wounded in battle.
7. A white Rhine wine. 8. Adam and Eve. 9. The pith of a plant.
10. Courage with the aid of strong liquor.

QUIZ 128

. . . .

1 St Francis de Sales is the patron saint of whom?

2 What kind of stew comes from Lancashire?

3 What were 'dundrearies'?

4 What kind of food item comes from Chelsea?

5 What kind of food is a garibaldi?

6 In cooking, what does en croûte mean?

7 From where does the popular pub name, 'The Pig and Whistle' come?

8 What are Quakers?

9 If you were a printer, how many points would make an inch?

10 If your birthday was April 5th, what star sign would you be?

ANSWERS

1. Authors and journalists. 2. Hot pot. 3. Long side-whiskers favoured in Victorian times. 4. A bun. 5. A kind of biscuit with a layer of currants. 6. Cooked in a pastry crust. 7. It was originally the Old English piggen wassail, a bucket from which drinkers filled their own mugs. 8. Followers of a belief put forward by George Fox, who rejected rites and creeds. 9. Twelve. 10. Aries.

QUIZ 129

• •

1 Which anniversary does a crystal wedding celebrate?

2 Who was the original Johnnie Walker of Scotch whisky fame?

3 What is Canasta?

4 St Jerome is the patron saint of whom?

5 St Elizabeth of Hungary is the patron saint of whom?

6 What are devils on horseback?

7 Which country's national assembly is called Congress?

8 Which are Europe's Latin languages?

9 If your surname is 'White', what might your nickname be?

10 According to the 'language of flowers', what does the quince signify?

ANSWERS

1. The fifteenth. 2. John Walker, an Ayrshire man, who bought a grocery business in Kilmarnock in 1820. 3. A card-game of the rummy family. 4. Librarians. 5. Bakers. 6. Prunes stuffed with chutney and grilled or fried rolled up in bacon. 7. The United States. 8. Italian, French, Spanish, Catalan, Portuguese, Romanian. 9. Snowy or Knocker. 10. Temptation.

QUIZ 130

. . . .

1 If your surname is 'Murphy', what might your nickname be?

2 What is Scientology?

3 Who was the first Pope?

4 How did worsted get its name?

5 What is prosciutto?

6 Who was James Earl Carter?

7 St Eloi is the patron saint of whom?

8 St Genesius is the patron saint of whom?

9 What is vermouth?

10 What is Shintoism?

ANSWERS

1. Spud. 2. A set of ideas put forward by a science-fiction writer, L. Ron Hubbard in the 1950s. 3. St Peter. 4. It was originally made in Worstead, Norfolk. 5. Finely-cured uncooked ham, often smoked. 6. Former US president Jimmy Carter. 7. Jewellers. 8. Actors. 9. A wine-based drink flavoured with herbs. 10. A Japanese form of Buddhism.

QUIZ 131

1 What does circa or c. in connection with dates mean?

2 In ancient times, what were centaurs believed to be?

3 What is a brandysnap?

4 The Palladium in London is a variety theatre. Isn't this a Latin name?

5 What was meant by 'my old Dutch'?

6 Which word, beginning with post- means 'after dinner'?

7 Who in the world would be called a 'Limey'?

8 Who or what was Big Bertha?

9 What, applied to a person, is a 'ham'?

10 Which politician is known as 'Tarzan'?

ANSWERS

1. About or around. 2. A race of beings half-horse, half-man. 3. A thin crisp biscuit flavoured with ginger and brandy. 4. Yes, but the original was a temple or image of the goddess Pallas. 5. A cockney expression, meaning 'my wife'. 6. Postprandial. 7. An Englishman. 8. A large gun trained on Paris during WW1. 9. An actor with more enthusiasm than ability. 10. Michael Heseltine.

QUIZ 132

• •

1 Who is the patron saint of travellers?

2 Who, or what, is 'Ernie'?

3 What is cannelloni?

4 What is a bisque?

5 What is haggis?

6 Who painted landscapes of the Suffolk countryside?

7 Which anniversary does a lace wedding celebrate?

8 What is a bruxelloise?

9 Moses was the leader of which nation?

10 What does the name of the city Philadelphia mean?

ANSWERS

1. St Christopher. 2. The Electronic Random Number Indicator Equipment for drawing Premium Bonds. 3. Thin rolls of pasta stuffed with meat or vegetables. 4. A creamy soup. 5. A Scottish dish made with the heart, lungs and liver of a sheep or calf. 6. John Constable. 7. The thirteenth. 8. A French sauce for asparagus. 9. Israel. 10. City of brotherly love.

QUIZ 133

• •

1   What are 'angels on horseback'?

2   Who was Sir Frank Brangwyn?

3   What is the name given to the male reproductive organ of a plant?

4   What had Shakespeare and George Washington in common?

5   What is a flapjack?

6   St Dunstan is the patron saint of whom?

7   A jeroboam is a measure of wine equivalent to how many bottles?

8   What is colcannon?

9   Who is the patron saint of Norway?

10 What are profiteroles?

ANSWERS

1. Oysters wrapped in bacon. 2. Artist, illustrator and designer. 3. The stamen. 4. They were both redheads. 5. A kind of broad, flat, pancake. 6. Blacksmiths. 7. Four. 8. An Irish dish of mashed potatoes and cabbage with butter. 9. St Olaf. 10. Small puffs of choux pastry, filled with cream and covered in chocolate sauce.

QUIZ 134

• •

1 If something is served à la maître d'hôtel, how is it prepared?

2 Osiris was a god of ancient Egypt. What was his domain?

3 What is pesto?

4 What is a sassenach?

5 What is a doughnut?

6 Which French liqueur has a strong anise taste?

7 Which anniversary does a china wedding celebrate?

8 Who was the Beast of Bolsover?

9 Who was Edith Cavell?

10 Who, in a music-hall song, went to Crewe in mistake for Birmingham?

ANSWERS

1. Served plain with parsley garnish. 2. The underworld. 3. A sauce of basil, garlic, pine nuts, olive oil and cheese. 4. An Englishman, according to the Scots language. 5. Sweetened dough, fried in fat. 6. Absinthe. 7. The twentieth. 8. Dennis Skinner, MP. 9. British nurse, executed by the Germans in WW1. 10. Marie Lloyd.

QUIZ 135

. . . .

1   What is meant by a 'ballpark figure'?

2   What does it signify when eight bells are sounded at sea?

3   St Anthony is the patron saint of whom?

4   Which anniversary does a steel wedding celebrate?

5   To the ancient Romans, who was Cupid?

6   What did Alexander of Macedon and Alfred, King of England, have in common?

7   What is another name for the 'Abominable Snowman'?

8   Who in the world would be called 'Digger'?

9   What did Oscar Wilde's Lady Windermere carry?

10 What kind of food is an Oval Osborne?

ANSWERS

1. A rough estimate. 2. The end of a watch of four hours. 3. Grave-diggers.
4. The eleventh. 5. The god of love. 6. They were both known by the title
'The Great'. 7. The Yeti. 8. An Australian. 9. A fan. 10. A kind of biscuit.

QUIZ 136

• •

1 What famous landmark stands on the site of Tyburn Tree in London?

2 Westminster Abbey is over 500 feet long. Yes or no?

3 What group of people are found in an orchestra?

4 What is meant by 'Dutch nightingales'?

5 What can be grouped into fleets?

6 In what place do Jewish people worship?

7 What is ratatouille?

8 The Goat represents which sign of the Zodiac?

9 What is mornay?

10 According to the 'language of flowers', what do oak leaves signify?

ANSWERS

1. Marble Arch. 2. Yes. It's 513 feet. 3. Musicians. 4. Frogs. 5. Ships, cars, birds. 6. A synagogue. 7. A vegetable stew containing tomatoes, aubergines, peppers, etc. 8. Capricorn. 9. A cream sauce with cheese flavouring. 10. Bravery.

QUIZ 137

1 How wide are the clock faces on the Clock Tower at Westminster: 23 feet, 25 feet or 30 feet?

2 Who is the patron saint of tax-collectors?

3 What is a Chateaubriand?

4 Which word, beginning with post- means 'after death?'

5 How much was a pennyweight?

6 What is a Battenburg?

7 Which theatre in London was originally called the Waldorf?

8 What is lasagne?

9 Friday is named after Frigga, the German goddess of married love. True or false?

10 What is the word for a group of angels?

ANSWERS

1. 23 feet. 2. St Matthew. 3. A thick grilled fillet steak. 4. Post-mortem. 5. 24 grains. 6. A cake with squares of pink and yellow sponge. 7. The Strand. 8. Flat pasta cooked with tomatoes, cheese or meat. 9. True. 10. A host.

QUIZ 138

1 What is a madeleine?

2 St Peter is the patron saint of whom?

3 Who was Alexander the Great?

4 What is kedgeree?

5 From the gastronomic point of view, what is a legume?

6 St Cecilia is the patron saint of whom?

7 St Stephen is the patron saint of whom?

8 What is bouillabaisse?

9 Which is London's largest park?

10 What is toad in the hole?

ANSWERS

1. A small, shell-shaped, sponge cake. 2. Fishermen. 3. A Macedonian soldier and conqueror who reached India. 4. A dish of rice, fish and hard-boiled eggs. 5. Peas, beans and lentils. 6. Singers and musicians.
7. Bricklayers. 8. A thick soup made with different kinds of fish.
9. Richmond, Surrey. 10. Sausages baked in batter.

QUIZ 139

. . . .

1 According to the 'language of flowers', what does the snowdrop signify?

2 Who is the patron saint of television?

3 What is euchre?

4 What is coleslaw?

5 What kind of food item comes from Melton Mowbray?

6 In the year 1752, what date followed 2nd September?

7 What is an agnostic?

8 What instrument did Niccolo Paganini play?

9 Which anniversary does a silk and fine linen wedding celebrate?

10 What is a referendum?

ANSWERS

1. Hope. 2. St Clare. 3. A card game. 4. A cabbage salad. 5. Meat pies.
6. 14th September. The calendar had changed and 11 days were omitted.
7. Someone who believes that man cannot know whether God exists or not. 8. The violin. 9. The twelfth. 10. A national vote on a particular issue.

QUIZ 140

1 What is couscous?

2 Who is the reigning monarch of Spain?

3 St Agatha is the patron saint of whom?

4 The American cartoonist Chester Gould conceived which character?

5 Which day is the Muslim Sabbath?

6 A Frenchman referring to 'trèfles, carreaux, piques, et coeurs' would be speaking of what?

7 According to the 'language of flowers', what does the veronica signify?

8 Sir William Alexander Smith founded what boys' organisation?

9 Some extra books to the Bible are called the Apocrypha. How many are there?

10 Whose capital is Edinburgh (apart from Scotland!)?

ANSWERS

1. A cereal dish of cracked grain or semolina. 2. Juan Carlos. 3. Nurses.
4. Dick Tracy. 5. Friday. 6. The suits of playing-cards. 7. Fidelity. 8. The Boys' Brigade. 9. Fifteen (all Old Testament). 10. Tristan da Cunha.

QUIZ 141

• •

1 A German referring to 'Herzen, Schellen, Grün und Eicheln' would be speaking of what?

2 What Italian artist was also an architect, philosopher, poet, composer, sculptor and mathematician?

3 To what did Buncombe, North Carolina, give its name?

4 Mercury is another name for the messenger of the gods Hermes. True or false?

5 What did Catherine II of Russia and Peter I of Russia have in common?

6 How old is the card game of Whist?

7 Which is the holy city of Hindus?

8 If something is held 'in camera', what does it mean?

9 What is béarnaise?

10 What is the Devil's Picture-book?

ANSWERS

1. German playing-cards with Hearts, Bells, Leaves and Acorns as suits.
2. Leonardo da Vinci. 3. Bunkum, or nonsense. 4. True. 5. They were both known by the title 'The Great'. 6. It dates from the eighteenth century.
7. Benares. 8. With the public as a whole excluded. 9. A sauce made with egg-yolks, butter, shallots, tarragon and vinegar. 10. A pack of playing-cards.

QUIZ 142

. . . .

1   In a pack of cards, which way does the Jack of Diamonds look, to his left, or to his right?

2   What is a vol au vent?

3   Which close relative of the onion has a similar, but more delicate flavour?

4   Which anniversary does a golden wedding celebrate?

5   What is the sixth sign of the Zodiac?

6   What, as a game, is Chemin de Fer?

7   Which anniversary does an iron or sugar-candy wedding celebrate?

8   What was a 'doughboy'?

9   What was a 'mae-west'?

10 Who in the world would be called a 'Pom' or 'Pommie'?

ANSWERS

1. To his left. 2. Very light puff pastry with room for a filling. 3. The leek.
4. The fiftieth. 5. Virgo. 6. A card game, mainly for gamblers. 7. The sixth.
8. An American soldier. 9. An inflatable life-jacket. 10. An Englishman, according to an Australian.

QUIZ 143

1   What food is junket?

2   Which anniversary does a silver wedding celebrate?

3   If your surname is 'Clark', what might your nickname be?

4   Who was the great love of Dante Alighieri?

5   Who ranks higher, a marquess or an earl?

6   What group of objects is described as a flotilla?

7   What is a dolma?

8   What was, or is, an Annie Oakley?

9   What is scrumpy?

10 Which anniversary does an ivory wedding celebrate?

ANSWERS

1. Curds, mixed with cream, sweetened and flavoured. 2. The twenty-fifth.
3. Nobby. 4. Beatrice. 5. A marquess. 6. Ships. 7. A vine or cabbage leaf with savoury stuffing. 8. A free ticket for a circus or theatre. 9. Cider made from small, sweet apples. 10. The fourteenth.

QUIZ 144

. . . .

1 What was called an 'Albert'?

2 The Bull represents which sign of the Zodiac?

3 Who composed 'The Planets'?

4 Rule by officialdom is called what?

5 According to the 'language of flowers', what does the bay leaf signify?

6 In a pack of cards, which way does the Jack of Hearts look, to his left, or to his right?

7 St Sebastian is the patron saint of whom?

8 Is a pantechnicon a large van?

9 Who was the first-ever murder victim?

10 St Isidore is the patron saint of whom?

ANSWERS

1. A heavy type of watch chain. 2. Taurus. 3. Gustave Holst.
4. A bureaucracy. 5. 'I change but in death'. 6. To his left. 7. Athletes.
8. It is now, but originally it was a building housing artistic works in Belgrave Square, London. 9. Abel, who was murdered by his brother, Cain.
10. Farmers.

QUIZ 145

• •

1 What, in Switzerland, are rappen?

2 What is baba au rhum?

3 The name of which naval hero is concealed by the anagram Honor est a Nilo?

4 St Raphael is the patron saint of whom?

5 What is an eclair?

6 Which anniversary does a bronze or electrical appliance wedding celebrate?

7 The Fishes represent which sign of the Zodiac?

8 What is a Mormon?

9 How did damask come to be named?

10 What does a Tarot pack of 78 cards comprise?

ANSWERS

1. The lowest value coins, also known as centimes. 2. A small cake, leavened with yeast, and soaked in a rum syrup. 3. Horatio Nelson. 4. Physicians. 5. A long, light pastry, covered with chocolate and filled with cream. 6. The eighth. 7. Pisces. 8. A religion founded in the United States by Joseph Smith in 1830. 9. It originated in Damascus. 10. Four suits each of 14, 21 permanent trumps and the Fool card.

QUIZ 146

• •

1   The Lion represents which sign of the Zodiac?

2   St Vitus is the patron saint of whom?

3   Is it true that Mormons are allowed several wives?

4   If your surname is 'Miller', what might your nickname be?

5   Of whom was Noël Coward speaking when he referred to 'Aunt Edna'?

6   The fava, or Windsor bean is better known as what?

7   Which word, beginning with post- means 'in the afternoon'?

8   What kind of food item comes from Yorkshire?

9   Name the first three who went to Widecombe Fair!

10 Name the second three who went to Widecombe Fair!

ANSWERS

1. Leo. 2. Comedians. 3. It was true, but the practice is no longer allowed.
4. Dusty. 5. A fictional audience character, typical of those attending
matinees. 6. The broad bean. 7. Post-meridian (usually shortenened to
p.m.). 8. Pudding. 9. Bill Brewer, Jan Stewer, Peter Gurney. 10. Peter Davy,
Dan'l Whidden, Harry Hawk.

QUIZ 147

• •

1 Who was the Yorkshire Ripper?

2 Who invented the lawnmower?

3 What is a 'romany rye'?

4 What kind of food item comes from Bakewell?

5 A legume with flat, dishlike seeds is called what?

6 Who was Honoré de Balzac?

7 St Lawrence is the patron saint of whom?

8 What kind of food was known as a 'wally'?

9 Which Sunday newspaper was first issued on 28th January, 1990

10 What did Mrs Mary Baker Eddy found?

ANSWERS

1. Peter Sutcliffe. 2. James Edward Ransome in 1902. 3. It is gypsy language, and means an outsider who joins them, learning their ways and language. 4. A tart. 5. Lentil. 6. French novelist. 7. Cooks. 8. A pickled gherkin. 9. The Independent on Sunday. 10. Christian Science.

QUIZ 148

1 Which anniversary does a china wedding celebrate?

2 What is a sorbet?

3 What is an atheist?

4 Which 19th-century event is concealed by the anagram I require love in a subject?

5 St Valentine is the patron saint of whom?

6 Which European princess had children named Albert, Caroline and Stephanie?

7 How many deadly sins are there?

8 Which anniversary does a coral wedding celebrate?

9 Who is the patron saint of wine-growers?

10 The river Medway runs through Kent. What is a man born east of it called?

ANSWERS

1. The twentieth. 2. A water-ice. 3. Someone who does not believe in a God. 4. Queen Victoria's Jubilee. 5. Lovers. 6. Princess Grace of Monaco. 7. Seven. 8. The thirty-fifth. 9. St Vincent. 10. A man of Kent.

QUIZ 149

. . . .

1 Which anniversary does a copper or pottery wedding celebrate?

2 The Ram represents which sign of the Zodiac?

3 What were, or are, the Gnomes of Zurich?

4 Which word, beginning with post- means 'published after the death of the composer or author'?

5 Indian ink didn't come from India. Where does it come from?

6 Who is the patron saint of sailors?

7 Dutch clocks didn't come from Holland. Where do they come from?

8 What is lobscouse?

9 Who, on stage in 1937, did the Lambeth Walk?

10 What does the abbreviation NATO stand for?

ANSWERS

1. The ninth. 2. Aries. 3. Swiss bankers and financiers. 4. Posthumous.
5. China. 6. St Cuthbert. 7. Germany. 8. An old seaman's dish of vegetables and sea-biscuit. 9. Lupino Lane. 10. North Atlantic Treaty Organisation.

QUIZ 150

1 What is the name given to the beam placed above a window or door?

2 In what place do Hindu people worship?

3 What did George Cruikshank do?

4 Turkish baths weren't started in Turkey. Where were they started?

5 In the Army who is more senior, a Major or a Colonel?

6 Which day is the Jewish Sabbath?

7 Who was Aubrey Beardsley?

8 Who was Karl Benz?

9 To the ancient Romans who was Venus?

10 What are marrons glacés?

ANSWERS

1. Lintel. 2. A temple. 3. He was a caricaturist and illustrator of books.
4. The Near East. 5. Colonel. 6. Saturday. 7. A black and white artist.
8. German maker of an early car. 9. The goddess of love. 10. Chestnuts coated with sugar.

QUIZ 151

• •

1   What kind of food item is associated with Bombay?

2   Who was Jean Renoir's father?

3   How many is a baker's dozen?

4   Who was Jesus?

5   What is the Trinity?

6   In a pack of cards, which way does the Jack of Spades look, to his left, or to his right?

7   According to the 'language of flowers', what does the jasmine signify?

8   Which daily newspaper was first published on 7th October, 1986?

9   What anniversary does a tin wedding celebrate?

10 Why is a bowler hat so called?

ANSWERS

1. Duck. It's not a duck at all, but a kind of fish. 2. Auguste Renoir.
3. Thirteen. 4. Christians believe he was the Son of God, and part of the Trinity. 5. The belief that God, Jesus and The Holy Spirit are all one. 6. To his left. 7. Amiability. 8. The Independent. 9. The tenth. 10. It was first sold by the hatters, Thomas and William Bowler.

QUIZ 152

• •

1 What is a prairie oyster?

2 Which American President was the last to be impeached?

3 What is a facade?

4 If you are a red-headed Australian, what might your nickname be?

5 What is gingerbread?

6 What is a 'blockbuster'?

7 What is abalone?

8 Which vitamin helps bone formation and keeps teeth healthy?

9 Which sign of the Zodiac represents the Virgin?

10 What is 'bubble and squeak'?

ANSWERS

1. A raw egg with vinegar and other condiments. 2. Richard Nixon. 3. The front of a building. 4. Bluey. 5. A cake flavoured with ginger and treacle. 6. A great success, as of a book, film or stage show. 7. A mollusc, like the sea snail, with a flat, oval shell. 8. Vitamin D. 9. Virgo. 10. A mashed, fried mixture of cabbage and potato.

QUIZ 153

• •

1   What anniversary does a flower or fruit wedding celebrate?

2   What is galantine?

3   To the ancient Greeks who was Pluto?

4   If you suffered from theophobia, what would you fear?

5   Which popular French drink contains wormwood oil?

6   What is a fondue?

7   Rule by a privileged class is called what?

8   Who invented the crossword puzzle?

9   St John of God is the patron saint of whom?

10 In which religion is the god Brahma found?

ANSWERS

1. The fourth. 2. A dish of poultry, veal, game, etc. served cold in a jelly.
3. The god of the dead. 4. God. 5. Absinthe. 6. A sauce made with cheese and wine, eaten by dipping pieces of bread or meat into it. 7. Aristocracy.
8. Arthur Wynne published the first one in the New York World in 1913.
9. Booksellers and publishers. 10. Hinduism.

QUIZ 154

• •

1. What is sauerkraut?

2. What is the Army equivalent of an Air Chief Marshal?

3. What is Cumberland sauce?

4. What was the occupation of Sir Jacob Epstein?

5. What anniversary does a woollen wedding celebrate?

6. What is stroganoff?

7. Who was Sheridan Morley's father?

8. Who was Thomas Arnold?

9. What was loo, as a game?

10. What word, beginning with post-, means 'a part added to a letter after the signature'?

ANSWERS

1. Cabbage fermented with salt. 2. General. 3. A redcurrant sauce with lemons, oranges, and port wine. 4. Sculptor. 5. The seventh. 6. Thinly-cut meat, onions and mushrooms in a sour cream sauce. 7. Robert Morley. 8. Famous headmaster of Rugby school. 9. A card game with many variants. 10. Postscript.

QUIZ 155

• •

1   Monday is named after the Moon. True or false?

2   Where in Britain would you find our oldest surviving clock?

3   What word, beginning with ante-, means 'before dinner'?

4   What is a Wiener schnitzel?

5   Who or what was Chad?

6   Who was Britain's answer to Louis Armstrong?

7   What was, or is, a billycock hat?

8   What is a Latter-Day Saint?

9   In a pack of cards, which way does the Queen of Diamonds look: to her left or to her right?

10 What anniversary does a wooden wedding celebrate?

ANSWERS

1. True. 2. Salisbury Cathedral, whose clock dates from 1386.
3. Anteprandial. 4. Veal cutlet covered in egg and breadcrumbs.
5. A little cartoon character who asked "Wot, no ......?" 6. Nat Gonella, who died in 1998 aged 90. 7. A bowler hat if you're British, a derby hat if you're American. 8. Another name for a Mormon. 9. To her left. 10. The fifth.

QUIZ 156

- -

1 If you asked for a 'biscuit' in the United States, what would you get?

2 What did American Express introduce in 1891?

3 What has been estimated at 50 million farenheit?

4 Who was the first 'Supermac'?

5 And which tennis player was the second 'Supermac'?

6 Who is Old Nick?

7 According to the 'language of flowers', what does the nasturtium signify?

8 What animal is grouped in packs?

9 If your surname is 'Martin', what might your nickname be?

10 In a pack of cards, which way does the King of Diamonds look, to his left, or to his right?

ANSWERS

1. A kind of scone. 2. Travellers' cheques. 3. The temperature at the centre of the sun. 4. Harold Macmillan. 5. John McEnroe. 6. Satan, or the Devil. 7. Patriotism. 8. Wolves. 9. Pincher. 10. To his right.

QUIZ 157

• •

1   What is 'Murphy's Law'?

2   What are duchesse potatoes?

3   What is laverbread?

4   What is a rissole?

5   What is a group of chickens called?

6   What is biltong?

7   Who was the 'Bouncing Czech'?

8   What did the S. stand for in the name of Harry S. Truman?

9   What is the Naval equivalent of a Field Marshal?

10   What is the London Palladium?

ANSWERS

1. Briefly, it says that 'what can go wrong, will go wrong. 2. Mashed potato, baked with butter, milk and egg-yolk. 3. Fronds of the porphyra seaweed, dipped in oatmeal and fried. 4. A fried meat ball or cake. 5. A brood.
6. Strips of dried lean meat from South Africa. 7. Robert Maxwell. 8. Nothing at all! 9. Admiral of the Fleet. 10. A famous theatre where top performers have appeared.

QUIZ 158

. . . .

1 Jews who in early times settled in Poland and Germany are called what?

2 The Archer represents which sign of the Zodiac?

3 Who's catchphrases included 'Nay, nay and thrice, nay'?

4 Who is the patron saint of tailors?

5 What was a 'penny gaff'?

6 The Isle of Portland, Dorset is not an island. What is it?

7 St Barbara is the patron saint of whom?

8 St Andrew is the patron saint of where?

9 What is perry?

10 What is a Bath bun?

ANSWERS

1. Ashkenazim. 2. Sagittarius. 3. English comedian, Frankie Howerd.
4. St Homobonus. 5. In Victorian times, a cheap, low-class music hall.
6. A peninsula. 7. Miners. 8. Scotland. 9. A drink made from fermented pear juice. 10. A rich, rather sweet, bun.

QUIZ 159

. . . .

1   What is béchamel?

2   What is fascism?

3   What, to a soldier, is a redcap?

4   Who was known as, 'the fifth Beatle'?

5   Turkeys didn't come from Turkey. Where did they originally come from?

6   The 'Abominable Snowman' is also known as?

7   What word, beginning with ante-, means 'before the existence of the world'?

8   Who is Allah?

9   Where did the orange originate?

10 What is gumbo?

ANSWERS

1. A white sauce flavoured with onion and herbs. 2. A system of government which has only one political party headed by a dictator. 3. A military policeman. 4. Producer, George Martin. 5. North America. 6. The Yeti. 7. Antemundane. 8. According to the Muslims, the Supreme Being, or God. 9. China. 10. A soup made with the okra plant.

QUIZ 160

• •

1 What word, beginning with post-, means 'to put off until a future time?'

2 Who in the world would be called a Canuck?

3 According to the 'language of flowers', what does the bluebell signify?

4 What is cock-a-leekie?

5 Who was Sir Malcolm Campbell?

6 How long have playing-cards been known in England; (a) 400 years (b) 500 years (c) 200 years?

7 In what place do Muslim people worship?

8 What group of people are referred to as a troupe?

9 Which English Admiral saw off the Spanish Armada?

10 Scorpions are immune to their own poison. True or false?

ANSWERS

1. Postpone. 2. A Canadian. 3. Constancy. 4. A soup made from a fowl and leeks. 5. Land-speed and water-speed record holder. 6. (a) 400 years. 7. A mosque. 8. Actors, acrobats, dancers, minstrels. 9. Sir Francis Drake. 10. False.

QUIZ 161

1 What is blutwurst?

2 Wednesday is named after Woden, the German god of war. True or false?

3 What is a Chelsea bun?

4 What is quiche?

5 What was 'ragtime'?

6 What is chilli con carne?

7 In a pack of cards, which way does the King of Clubs look, to his left, or to his right?

8 Who was Albrecht Dürer?

9 What are 'Grape Nuts' and who invented them?

10 What does LBW stand for?

ANSWERS

1. The German version of black pudding. 2. True. 3. A rolled bun filled with currants and raisins. 4. A shell of unsweetened pastry which can hold a savoury filling. 5. A type of very POP MUSIC which preceded jazz. 6. Minced meat, beans and chillis. 7. To his right. 8. A German painter and engraver. 9. A breakfast cereal invented by Charles Post in 1898. 10. Leg Before Wicket in cricket.

QUIZ 162

• •

1 St Anne is the patron saint of whom?

2 Who is the patron saint of shoemakers?

3 Where does the word 'patter', meaning stage 'chat', come from?

4 In a pack of cards, which way does the King of Spades look, to his left, or to his right?

5 What word, beginning with ante-, means 'in the time before the war'?

6 From an edible point of view, what are bullseyes?

7 What does ROM stand for in computing?

8 What items are called by names such as Plantin, Baskerville and Garamond?

9 What is a tortilla?

10 Who was Tommy Atkins?

ANSWERS

1. Housewives. 2. St Crispin. 3. From the name of the Our Father prayer in Latin, Paternoster. 4. To his left. 5. Antebellum. 6. Round, hard, black-and-white striped peppermint-flavoured sweets. 7. Read Only Memory. 8. Printers' typefaces. 9. A Spanish omelette of potato and egg; also a Mexican maize pancake. 10. A typical British soldier.

QUIZ 163

. . . .

1 Which British exponent of jazz on radio died very recently?

2 What is chowder?

3 A magnum is a measure of wine equivalent to how many bottles?

4 What does 'kosher' mean?

5 What is the second most expensive property on a Monopoly board?

6 Why 'dead as a doornail'?

7 Who is Viscount Linley's mother?

8 St Thomas is the patron saint of whom?

9 What is a hot dog?

10 What is a fricassee?

ANSWERS

1. Benny Green. 2. A thick soup made from meat or fish. 3. Two. 4. Fit to be eaten according to Jewish law. 5. Park Lane. 6. A door nail is the bit which is whacked by the knocker. 7. Princess Margaret. 8. Architects.
9. A frankfurter inside a long soft bun. 10. A dish of cut pieces of fowl or meat, cooked in a sauce.

QUIZ 164

. . . .

1 On which radio programme would you find CMJ, Blowers and Fred?

2 St Vincent Ferrer is the patron saint of whom?

3 What is housed at Hertford House in London?

4 What is risotto?

5 Which musician was known as 'Flash Harry'?

6 Rule by an hereditary monarch in his or her own right is called what?

7 St George is the patron saint of where?

8 How does the Archbishop of Canterbury sign himself?

9 What kind of food item comes from Kendal?

10 What's the connection between baloney and polony?

ANSWERS

1. Test Match Special. 2. Builders. 3. The Wallace Collection. 4. Rice cooked in stock, with meat, saffron, vegetables and cheese. 5. Sir Malcolm Sargent. 6. A monarchy. 7. England. 8. His name, followed by Cantuar. 9. A mint cake. 10. From the Bologna sausage: the first means 'rubbish, nonsense', and the second is the sausage (US version).

QUIZ 165

1 What is cassata?

2 What is poker?

3 What anniversary does a diamond wedding celebrate?

4 What word, beginning with ante- means 'going before, in time'?

5 What is bratwurst?

6 The Water Carrier represents which sign of the Zodiac?

7 What is a Bar Mitzvah?

8 St Michael is the patron saint of whom?

9 Whose motto is: 'E Pluribus Unum'?

10 Chips with Everything was a successful play by which author?

ANSWERS

1. Italian ice-cream with layers of fruit and nuts. 2. A card-game which involves clever thinking, but is basically for gamblers. 3. The sixtieth, and also the seventy-fifth. 4. Antecedent. 5. A German fat pork sausage. 6. Aquarius. 7. A confirmation ceremony for Jewish boys when they reach the age of 13. 8. Soldiers. 9. The United States of America. 10. Arnold Wesker.

QUIZ 166

• •

1　What does 'to bellyache' mean?

2　Where did the Flintstones live?

3　What does 'beef up' mean?

4　What is an ampersand?

5　What does the expression 'in the can' mean?

6　What were 'Teddy Boys'?

7　What is a 'Hooray Henry'?

8　What does 'in the buff' mean?

9　What is a 'sleuth'?

10　What is a 'shemozzle'?

ANSWERS

1. To complain. 2. Bedrock. 3. To strengthen or reinforce. 4. The symbol & meaning 'and'. 5. Something has been successfully accomplished. 6. Gangs of young lads who wore long jackets and narrow trousers. 7. An upper-class twit with an affected accent. 8. Naked. 9. A detective. 10. A mess, row or rumpus.

QUIZ 167

. . . .

1 What, according to the old schoolboys' joke, is the meaning of coup de grâce?

2 What, to a British soldier, was 'Blighty'?

3 If you were 'in the altogether', what would you be?

4 If you asked the price, and were told 'gratis', what would you pay?

5 Who made the phrase, 'Clunk, Click - Every Trip' famous?

6 Which comic featured the characters, Biffa Bacon, Billy The Fish and Black Bag?

7 In American English, what is a 'rubberneck'?

8 What is, or was, a spoonerism?

9 What is a busker?

10 If you were in the Army, and 'got a rocket', what would have happened?

ANSWERS

1. A lawn-mower. 2. Home. 3. Naked. 4. Nothing! 5. Jimmy Savile. 6. Viz. 7. Someone who stares and gawps. 8. A habit of transposing initial letters of words, as 'shoving leopard' for 'loving shepherd. 9. A street singer or performer. 10. You would have received a severe telling-off.

QUIZ 168

1 What does 'naff' mean?

2 If someone sent you an invitation marked R.S.V.P., what should you do?

3 Why were the first London policemen called 'peelers'?

4 What does AWOL stand for?

5 What does 'schmaltz' mean?

6 What was nicknamed 'The Thunderer'?

7 What did the Owl and the Pussycat go to sea in?

8 What is The Observer?

9 By what name is Robert Louis Stevenson's novel, The Sea Cook better known?

10 In the 1930s, a child could buy The Rainbow. What was it?

ANSWERS

1. It describes something inferior or below standard. 2. Make sure you reply! 3. They were first organised by Sir Robert Peel. 4. Absent WithOut Leave. 5. Sickly sweet, sentiment. 6. The Times newspaper. 7. A beautiful pea green boat. 8. A long-established Sunday newspaper. 9. Treasure Island. 10. A weekly children's comic.

QUIZ 169

1 Who, or what, is Stanley Gibbons?

2 Where and what was Dixieland?

3 What was a 'Tin Lizzie'?

4 What does 'carry coals to Newcastle' mean?

5 What is the Reader's Digest?

6 Who created 'Tarzan'?

7 What is Private Eye?

8 What is the Frankfurter Allgemeine Zeitung? Is it
   (a) a newpaper (b) a sausage (c) a secret society?

9 What famous book did A.A. Milne write?

10 Which country was the home of Dracula?

ANSWERS

1. A famous London stamp dealer. 2. The Southern States of America.
3. An early Ford car. 4. To do a pointless, useless task. 5. A monthly
magazine specialising in extracts from other sources. 6. Edgar Rice
Burroughs. 7. A weekly satirical newspaper. 8. (a) A newspaper. 9. Winnie
the Pooh. 10. Transylvania.

QUIZ 170

• •

1 St Michael is the patron saint of whom?

2 If you go back 20 years or so, who would measure something in picas?

3 The jolly swagman went 'Waltzing Matilda'. What was a matilda?

4 Can you eat acorns?

5 St Nicholas is the patron saint of whom?

6 Of what group does one find a posse?

7 Which herb looks like parsley but has a slight taste of aniseed?

8 Who was the painter of the famous Laughing Cavalier?

9 Who is the patron saint of scholars?

10 In which city, apart from London, would you find Soho?

ANSWERS

1. Grocers. 2. A printer. A pica is one-sixth of an inch. 3. The swagman's roll containing his blanket. 4. Yes, but they are better served up as food for pigs. 5. Children. 6. Cowboys, constables, police. 7. Chervil. 8. The Dutch portrait painter, Frans Hals. 9. St Bridget. 10. Birmingham.

QUIZ 171

. . . .

1   What is kohlrabi?

2   The name of which famous nurse is concealed by the anagram Flit on, cheering angel?

3   Who in the world would be called a 'Jock'?

4   In a pack of cards, which way does the Queen of Spades look: to her left, or to her right?

5   What are the religious followers of Nanak called?

6   What do O.J. Simpson's initials stand for?

7   St David is the patron saint of whom?

8   Who was the 'Brown Bomber'?

9   What is Albert sauce?

10 Who in the world would be called a 'Kraut'?

ANSWERS

1. A variety of cabbage, but much like a turnip. 2. Florence Nightingale.
3. A Scotsman. 4. To her right. 5. Sikhs. 6. Orenthal James. 7. Poets.
8. Joe Louis, heavyweight boxer. 9. A sauce made with cream, butter, horse-radish, mustard and vinegar. 10. A German.

QUIZ 172

• •

1   Who was the Father of English Poetry?

2   Which anniversary does an emerald wedding celebrate?

3   What kind of food is baclava?

4   According to the 'language of flowers', what does the honeysuckle signify?

5   Poseidon is another name for Neptune. True or false?

6   What is the Koran?

7   What is a male swan called?

8   Who, or what, in London, is the 'Old Bill'?

9   What is Dogget's Coat and Badge?

10 To the ancient Romans, who was Jupiter?

ANSWERS

1. Geoffrey Chaucer. 2. The fifty-fifth. 3. Pastry filled with nuts and honey.
4. Generous and devoted attention. 5. True. 6. The sacred book of Islam.
7. A cob. 8. The Metropolitan Police. 9. A prize annually awarded to Thames watermen. 10. The god ruling all gods and men.

QUIZ 173

• •

1 What is a Christian Scientist?

2 What is the Talmud?

3 In wartime, what was a WAAF?

4 What is a kebab?

5 What is Bezique?

6 What is nougat?

7 What does the Beaufort Scale measure?

8 Who was 'Tricky Dicky'?

9 Which tribal chieftain in Europe became president and later, king of his country?

10 What is a prune?

ANSWERS

1. Someone who believes that healing can be achieved by religious faith.
2. An encyclopaedia of Jewish laws. 3. A member of the Women's Auxiliary Air Force. 4. Vegetables, meats, etc., cooked on a skewer. 5. A card-game which originated in France. 6. A sweetmeat, of a sweet paste filled with chopped nuts. 7. Winds. 8. US President Richard Nixon. 9. Zog of Albania. 10. A dried plum.

QUIZ 174

• •

1 St Luke is the patron saint of whom?

2 What is Islam?

3 What is a thick cream of lemon juice, lemon peel, eggs, sugar and butter called?

4 Which word, beginning with ante- means 'to date, before true time'?

5 Two 16th-century German painters, father and son, had the same name. Who were they?

6 Composed of what group does one find a bevy?

7 Who was Sir Stafford Cripps?

8 What animal's name do the Chinese give to the year 1999?

9 Thursday is named after Thor, the German god of thunder. True or false?

10 Sunday is named after the Sun. True or false?

ANSWERS

1. Doctors. 2. The religion founded by Muhammad 1,300 years ago.
3. Lemon curd. 4. Antedate. 5. Hans Holbein, the Elder and the Younger.
6. Girls, beauty, larks, quails, swans. 7. British Labour statesman and
Chancellor of the Exchequer. 8. The year of the Hare. 9. True. 10. True.

QUIZ 175

• •

1 To the ancient Greeks and Romans who was Apollo?

2 Who was the original 'Angry Young Man'?

3 How did teddy-bears receive their name?

4 If you were born on Good Friday or Christmas Day, what special power might you have?

5 If a foreign car displayed the letters RO, what would its country of origin be?

6 The Crab represents which sign of the Zodiac?

7 What is the Society of Friends?

8 St Jude is the patron saint of what?

9 What is a macaroon?

10 Which word, beginning with post- means 'someone who studies after graduating'?

ANSWERS

1. The god of music and poetry. 2. John Osborne. 3. It was named after the American president, Theodore 'Teddy' Roosevelt. 4. The power of seeing and commanding spirits! 5. Romania. 6. Cancer. 7. Another name for the Quakers. 8. Lost causes. 9. A sweet biscuit made with almonds. 10. Postgraduate.

QUIZ 176

1 Who painted the picture of a stag entitled 'Monarch of the Glen'?

2 What is an éclair?

3 The Scales represent which sign of the Zodiac?

4 Which anniversary does a cotton wedding celebrate?

5 What is an ambassador?

6 What group of objects can be described as a crew?

7 What kind of food item comes from Banbury?

8 Who was Britain's monarch before Queen Elizabeth II?

9 What group is often described as a fifteen?

10 Who was Konrad Adenauer?

ANSWERS

1. Sir Edwin Landseer. 2. A long, light pastry with cream filling and chocolate sauce. 3. Libra. 4. The first. 5. A diplomatic envoy who represents his own head of state in a foreign country. 6. Sailors or aircraft staff. 7. Cake. A kind of mince pie. 8. George VI. 9. A rugby team. 10. A German statesman.

QUIZ 177

. . . .

1   What is meant by 'Dutch gold'?

2   What is consommé?

3   What kind of food item comes from Worcester?

4   What is the name of the young girl who plays a
leading part in Peter Pan?

5   How does the Archbishop of York sign himself?

6   Which word, beginning with post- means 'those
coming after'?

7   Who is the reigning monarch in Denmark?

8   St Apollonia is the patron saint of whom?

9   Which anniversary does a paper wedding
celebrate?

10 What is black pudding?

ANSWERS

1. An alloy of copper and zinc. 2. Clear meat soup. 3. Sauce. 4. Wendy. 5. His
Christian name followed by Ebor. 6. Posterity. 7. Queen Margaret II.
8. Dentists. 9. The second. 10. A kind of sausage made from pigs' blood.

QUIZ 178

. . . .

1 In a pack of cards, which way does the Queen of Clubs look: to her left, or to her right?

2 Who is the reigning monarch of Japan?

3 Eros is another name for Cupid. True or false?

4 Rule by the people as a whole is called what?

5 What is a 'Scotch woodcock'?

6 Jews who in early times settled in Spain and Portugal are called what?

7 If you suffered from ombrophobia, what would you fear?

8 What is gazpacho?

9 Who was Jean-Baptiste Corot?

10 Of what group does one find a sheaf?

ANSWERS

1. To her left. 2. Emperor Akihito. 3. True. 4. Democracy. 5. Eggs and anchovies on toast. 6. Sephardim. 7. Rainstorms. 8. A spicy Spanish vegetable dish, served cold. 9. French landscape painter. 10. Arrows, papers, corn.

QUIZ 179

. . . .

1   From which musical play did the song 'Some Day
    My Heart Will Awake' come?

2   What is saltimbocca?

3   Which British stamps were the first to be
    perforated?

4   Who was the Boston Strangler?

5   'Shear you sheep in May….' (what's the next line
    in the verse?)

6   How was 'mayonnaise' named?

7   To the ancient Romans, who was Mars?

8   What is a paella?

9   What kind of food is a custard-cream?

10 Which musical play featured the song 'Climb Ev'ry
    Mountain'?

ANSWERS

1. King's Rhapsody. 2. An Italian dish of veal, ham and cheese. 3. The Penny
Red of 1854. 4. Albert de Salvo. 5. 'And shear them all away'. 6. It was first
used at the port of Mahón, Minorca, and named after it. 7. The god of war.
8. A dish of meat with saffron rice and seafood. 9. A kind of sandwich
biscuit with a centre layer of cream. 10. The Sound of Music.

QUIZ 180

• •

1 In a pack of cards, which way does the Jack of Clubs look: to his left, or to his right?

2 The Twins represent which sign of the Zodiac?

3 What does 'Going Dutch' mean?

4 What is a tartare sauce?

5 The lemon-sole is not a sole, but a relative of what?

6 What are gnocchi?

7 Who is the reigning prince of Luxembourg?

8 St Fiacre is the patron saint of whom?

9 According to the 'language of flowers', what does the peony signify?

10 What suits are found in a traditional pack of Tarot cards?

ANSWERS

1. To his right. 2. Gemini. 3. Each person paying for themselves at a meal. 4. A mayonnaise dressing with chopped pickles, olives, capers etc. 5. The plaice. 6. Italian savoury dumplings. 7. Jean. 8. Cab-drivers. 9. Shame or bashfulness. 10. The Italian suits of Batons, Swords, Coins and Cups.

QUIZ 181

• •

1 In which year did Britain join the EEC?

2 Whose statue stands in front of Wesley's Chapel in City Road, London?

3 What kind of food product is aioli?

4 What is chow mein?

5 Samson, a judge of Israel, possessed what great gift?

6 Who would be taking the advice 'vamp till ready'?

7 Who is Ken Dodd?

8 Which architect designed Waterloo Bridge and the present Anglican Cathedral in Liverpool?

9 St Augustine is the patron saint of whom?

10 What is doner kebab?

ANSWERS

1. 1972. 2. John Wesley. 3. Garlic mayonnaise. 4. Fried noodles. 5. Enormous strength. 6. A piano accompanist. 7. A Lancashire comedian. 8. Sir Giles Gilbert Scott. 9. Brewers. 10. Thin slices of seasoned lamb grilled on a spit.

QUIZ 182

1 Who in the world would be called 'Taffy'?

2 What is an 'idiot board'?

3 Who is the patron saint of sculptors?

4 What anniversary does a leather wedding celebrate?

5 In ancient times what was King Midas's big problem?

6 What is a pizza?

7 A clutch is composed of what items?

8 In British movies and on stage, which actress was famed for her portrayal of eccentric elderly ladies?

9 What is paté de fois gras?

10 Who is the patron saint of secretaries?

ANSWERS

1. A Welshman. 2. A card used in a television studio to prompt an actor.
3. St Claude. 4. The third. 5. Everything he touched turned to gold. 6. An open pie of bread dough, with various toppings. 7. Eggs. 8. Margaret Rutherford. 9. Goose liver pâté. 10. St Cassian

QUIZ 183

• •

1 Who is the patron saint of workers?

2 What creature is sometimes known as 'Devil's Fingers'?

3 What are blinis or blintzis?

4 What word, beginning with ante-, means 'a small room leading to another'?

5 What is cribbage?

6 What is the name given to a lake of sea water bounded by a coral reef?

7 What anniversary does a ruby wedding celebrate?

8 What is a kipper?

9 What food comes from Eccles in Lancashire?

10 St Augustine of Hippo is the patron saint of whom?

ANSWERS

1. St Joseph. 2. The starfish. 3. Russian thin, stuffed pancakes. 4. Anteroom.
5. A card game for a varying number of players. 6. Lagoon. 7. The fortieth.
8. A smoked herring. 9. A cake. 10. Printers.

QUIZ 184

• •

1   St Nicholas is the patron saint of whom?

2   In cricket who is the Twelfth Man?

3   Who was Boofy Gore?

4   To the ancient Romans who was Saturn?

5   What is meant by 'Dutch comfort'?

6   What did Albert Schweitzer set up in Lambaréné?

7   What is the Army equivalent of a Lieutenant Commander in the Navy?

8   How did 'knickers' get their name?

9   A methuselah is a measure of wine equivalent to how many bottles?

10 What article of clothing is a mantilla?

ANSWERS

1. Bakers. 2. The substitute. 3. 8th Earl of Arran, politician and journalist.
4. The god of agriculture. 5. Cold comfort. 6. A hospital to combat leprosy.
7. Major. 8. From Knickerbocker, a character in a Washington Irving book,
who wore knee-length breeches. 9. Eight. 10. A kind of lace cap worn in
Spain.

QUIZ 185

1 What is stingo?

2 What is smörgåsbord?

3 What is a ragout?

4 Whalebone isn't the bone of a whale. What is it?

5 In card-playing, how did the word 'trump' come into being?

6 What word, beginning with ante- means 'before midday'?

7 What was Dr. Who's time machine called?

8 What is charlotte russe?

9 According to the 'language of flowers', what does the foxglove signify?

10 What is halva?

ANSWERS

1. Strong malt liquor. 2. A Swedish hors d'œuvres dish. 3. A highly-seasoned stew of meat and vegetables. 4. A horny substance from the whale's jaw. 5. It was taken from the word 'triumph'. 6. Ante meridian. 7. The TARDIS. 8. A sponge-cake containing cream, biscuit and flavourings. 9. Insincerity. 10. A sweet made with sesame seeds and honey.

QUIZ 186

• •

1 Saturday is named after Saturn, the Roman god of culture and vegetation. True or false?

2 Which artist was renowned for his paintings of horses?

3 Which Dutch liqueur is sometimes called 'egg brandy'?

4 St Christopher is the patron saint of whom?

5 What word, beginning with ante-, means 'before birth'?

6 St Joseph is the patron saint of whom?

7 What were Lyons' Corner Houses?

8 Heracles is another name for Hercules. True or false?

9 What word, beginning with ante- means 'before, in time or place'?

10 What had Queen Victoria and Harpo Marx in common?

ANSWERS

1. True. 2. George Stubbs. 3. Advocaat. 4. Travellers. 5. Antenatal.
6. Carpenters. 7. Large restaurants in London where the cost of entertainment was within reach of ordinary people. 8. True. 9. Anterior.
10. They were both left-handed.

QUIZ 187

• •

1 In a pack of cards, which way does the Queen of Hearts look, to her left, or to her right?

2 What is chop suey?

3 What is pumpernickel?

4 What are crêpes suzettes?

5 In Britain, we had the game ninepins. The Americans have tenpins. Why?

6 R. Harmenzoon van Rijn was one of the most famous of all painters. What does the R stand for?

7 St Patrick is the patron saint of what?

8 What is the Fabian Society?

9 St Amand is the patron saint of whom?

10 What type of entertainment is a 'Charleston'?

ANSWERS

1. To her right. 2. A US-invented Chinese dish usually containing beansprouts. 3. A coarse, malted rye bread. 4. Thin, hot pancakes with lemons or oranges. 5. Ninepins was banned in America. Using the extra pin got around the law. 6. Rembrandt. 7. Ireland. 8. A socialist group founded in 1884. 9. Innkeepers and wine-merchants. 10. A type of dance.

QUIZ 188

• •

1   St John Bosco is the patron saint of whom?

2   What year was the Battle of Britain?

3   If you were rudely called a coot, what is it likely you'll be?

4   The first public restaurant was opened in 1765 in what city?

5   Name two well-known plays by Terence Rattigan.

6   What is the maximum break in snooker?

7   What is borsht?

8   Who is the Pope?

9   What word, beginning with ante,- means 'existing before the Great Flood'?

10 Where is the Golden Gate?

ANSWERS

1. Editors. 2. 1940. 3. Bald. 4. Paris. 5. Flare Path, French Without Tears, While
6. 147. 7. Russian beetroot soup. 8. The head of the Roman Catholic
Church. 9. Antediluvian. 10. The entrance to the bay of San Francisco.

QUIZ 189

. . . .

1 What did athlete Darren Campbell win in the 1998 European Championships?

2 What are a Manhattan and a Screwdriver?

3 The titmouse isn't a mouse. What is it?

4 Who is the patron saint of scientists?

5 What are 'petits fours'?

6 What is Yom Kippur?

7 What were Pioneer, Galileo and Magellan?

8 A stitch in time will save how many?

9 St Boniface is the patron saint of what?

10 The impresario Lewis Winogradsky is better known as whom?

ANSWERS

1. A Gold Medal in the 100m. 2. Cocktails. 3. A small bird. 4. St Albert.
5. Small, very fancy, biscuits or cakes. 6. The Jewish Day of Atonement.
7. Space probes. 8. Nine. 9. Germany. 10. Lord Grade.

QUIZ 190

● ●

1   If you went by Shanks's pony, how would you be travelling?

2   What is 'plonk'?

3   What is an 'Oscar'?

4   If someone asked you to be QUEBEC UNIFORM INDIA ECHO TANGO what would you have to do?

5   What does 'above board' mean?

6   What is 'Adam's ale'?

7   What does the symbol © mean?

8   What is an 'oik'?

9   If, in the Navy, the captain gave the order 'splice the mainbrace', what would happen?

10 What's a 'Walter Mitty'?

ANSWERS

1. On foot. 2. Cheap wine; a term originating in Australia. 3. An Academy Award in the film business. 4. Be quiet! 5. Honest, genuine. 6. Water. 7. Copyright. 8. An ignorant lout. 9. All sailors received an extra tot of rum. 10. A day-dreaming fantasist.

QUIZ 191
QUESTIONS FROM THE SIXTIES

1 Which sportsman's nickname was "Broadway Joe"?

2 Who played Blofeld in You Only Live Twice?

3 What colour was his cat?

4 In which country was poet Peter Porter born?

5 Which future political heavyweight was working for the National Union of Seamen in 1968?

6 For which TV show did Allan Plater write many scripts?

7 Which Eastbourne doctor suspected of killing his patients was reinstated by the Medical Council in 1961?

8 Who joined BBC Radio in 1969, with a degree in Scandinavian studies?

9 Which field marshal and adviser to Churchill died in 1963?

10 Whom did Angus Ogilvy marry in 1963?

ANSWERS

1. Joe Namath 2. Donald Pleasence 3. White 4. Australia 5. John Prescott
6. Z Cars 7. John Bodkin Adams 8. Kate Adie 9. Viscount Alanbrooke
10. Princess Alexandra

QUIZ 192

QUESTIONS FROM THE SIXTIES

1 What did the Pope tell Catholics not to watch if the Vatican judged them "unsafe"?

2 Which bridegroom-to-be was the son of the Countess of Rosse?

3 What did aviation minister Duncan Sandys say Britain would build?

4 Where were private businesses nationalized?

5 Which royal prince was born on 19 February?

6 What were his full names?

7 In which continent was Nyasaland?

8 What invention of 1960 was credited to Theodore Maiman?

9 In which English county was the Jodrell Bank radio telescope built?

ANSWERS

1. Television programmes 2. Antony Armstrong-Jones 3. A supersonic airliner 4. Cuba 5. Prince Andrew 6. Andrew Albert Christian Edward 7. Africa 8. The laser 9. Cheshire 10. Charlton Heston

QUIZ 193
QUESTIONS FROM THE SIXTIES

1 Which Irish politician said (allegedly) "What we need is another Cromwell"?

2 Whose wife was Queen Fabiola?

3 Who said: "Politicians promise to build a bridge when there is no river"?

4 Which Archbishop of Canterbury met the Pope in December 1960?

5 Which British actress played Katherine in The Taming of the Shrew at Stratford?

6 Which country launched its first space rocket in January 1961?

7 Which famous animal died in Kenya in 1961?

8 Which British car reached the "1 million made" mark in 1965?

9 What speed became the legal maximum on British roads in 1965?

10 What slogan was used to promote British goods and businesses during 1969–70?

ANSWERS

1, Ian Paisley 2, King Baudouin of the Belgians 3, Khrushchev 4, Dr Geoffrey Fisher 5, Peggy Ashcroft 6, Italy 7, Elsa the lioness 8, The Mini 9, 70 mph 10, I'm backing Britain

QUIZ 194

QUESTIONS FROM THE SIXTIES

1 What was Donald Crowhurst doing when he disappeared in 1969?

2 Which two countries fought a "Soccer War"?

3 In what year?

4 Which star of the 1963 epic Cleopatra wore 65 costumes?

5 Which London landmark was cleaned in 1968, for the first time since 1844?

6 By what name was detective writer "Nicholas Blake" better known?

7 Whcih defence organization was disbanded in 1968?

8 Who played the photographer in Blow Up?

9 What were there 3.4 billion of in 1967?

10 Which stretch of water did John Fairfax row in 1969?

ANSWERS

1, Taking part in a round the world yacht race 2, El Salvador and Honduras 3, 1969 4, Elizabeth Taylor 5, Nelson's Column 6, Cecil Day-Lewis 7, The Civil Defence Corps in Britain 8, David Hemmings 9, People in the world 10, The Atlantic Ocean

QUIZ 195

QUESTIONS FROM THE SIXTIES

1 What ran for the last time on 11 August 1968 in Britain?

2 Whose widow was Princess Marina, who died in 1968?

3 What was the name of Britain's first nuclear submarine?

4 For which crime was Ronald Biggs convicted in 1964?

5 Which river became associated with a pop music sound in the early 60s?

6 What year was the Cuban missile crisis?

7 Which new British cathedral was consecrated in 1962?

8 What year did "Apollo 12" land on the Moon?

9 What was Colin Cowdrey's first name?

10 Which southern African country became independent in 1968?

ANSWERS

1, Steam trains 2, The Duke of Kent's 3, "Dreadnought" 4, His part in the Great Train Robbery of 1963 5, The Mersey ("Merseybeat") 6, 1962 7, Coventry 8, 1969 (November) 9, Michael 10, Swaziland

QUIZ 196

QUESTIONS FROM THE SIXTIES

1 Japan's Kobe Zoo bred a leopon in 1969. What was this animal?

2 What was the "Amsterdam", uncovered in 1969?

3 Where was it found?

4 Why did dogs pull Mounties for the last time in 1969?

5 What was Cilla Black's job at the Cavern Club when she was spotted by John Lennon?

6 At which Welsh singer was it not unusual for female fans to hurl their knickers on-stage?

7 Which organization celebrated its 50th birthday on 1 April 1968?

8 What kind of sport went on at Germany's Nurburgring?

9 In what part of the world was the Crater district a dangerous place to be in 1967?

10 Why did the "Torrey Canyon" hit the headlines in 1967?

ANSWERS

1, A cross between a male leopard and a female lion 2, An 18th-century Dutch ship 3, Offshore from Hastings, England 4, The Royal Canadian Mounted Police made its last spring patrol with dog sleds 5, She was a hat-check girl 6, Tom Jones 7, The Royal Air Force 8, Motor racing 9, Aden (at the time of terrorist campaign) 10, It was an oil tanker that created a major oil spill

QUIZ 197
QUESTIONS FROM THE SIXTIES

1 In what activity did Vidal Sassoon make his name?

2 Which British coin ceased to be legal tender in 1960?

3 What year was the Aberfan disaster in South Wales?

4 What year was Britain's first credit card introduced?

5 Why was Red Alligator in the news in 1968?

6 Who were the last to be called up in 1960?

7 Peter Dawson died in 1960; was he a) a singer b) a comedian
   c) a cricketer?

8 And was he a) Scottish b) Irish or c) Australian?

9 Hardy Amies designed what for the Queen: a) clothes b) gardens
   c) yachts?

10 What local government was replaced by the GLC?

ANSWERS

1, Hairdressing 2, The farthing 3, 1966 4, 1966 (Barclaycard) 5, It won the Grand National horse race 6, National servicemen 7, a) A singer 8, c) Australian 9, a) Clothes 10, The old London County Council

QUIZ 198
QUESTIONS FROM THE SIXTIES

1 Who recorded a song called Love Me Do in 1962?

2 Was Brian Kidd a) a pop singer b) a soccer player c) prime minister of New Zealand?

3 Jean Shrimpton was a famous 60s … a) singer b) model c) film star?

4 Why was James Meredith turned away from university in 1962?

5 Was The Monster Mash of 1962 a hit song, a food craze, or a giant earth-mover?

6 What was unusual about the Whiskey A-Go-Go of 1963?

7 Among its attractions were a) dancers in cages, b) lap dancers c) girls jumping out of giant bottles?

8 He was Shane Fenton in the 60s; by what name was he better known in the 70s?

9 Which Scottish loch was in the news when US nuclear submarines were based there?

10 Which pop singer became father to a daughter named Kim in 1960?

ANSWERS

1, The Beatles 2, b) he played for Man Utd 3, b) Model 4, He was a black student seeking admission to a segregated college in Mississippi, USA 5, "A song, by Bobby "Boris" Pickett and The Crypt-Kickers 6, First disco on Los Angeles' Sunset Boulevard 7, a) Dancers in cages 8, Alvin Stardust 9, Holy Loch 10, Marty Wilde

QUIZ 199
QUESTIONS FROM THE SIXTIES

1 Which Scottish actor made the headlines as Hamlet in 1969?

2 Which US city elected the same mayor three times in the 60s?

3 Who was the mayor?

4 Which corporation did Lee Iacocca head for a time?

5 Whom did Princess Sophia of Greece marry?

6 Of which country was Simon Kapepwe vice-president?

7 Who succeeded Michael Stewart as British Foreign Secretary in 1966?

8 What did the US lose over the Atlantic in 1966?

9 What first did Edward Brooke achieve in 1966?

10 What did France pull out of in 1966?

ANSWERS

1, Nicol Williamson 2, New York City 3, Sam Yorty 4, Ford Motor Co.
5, Prince Juan Carlos of Spain 6, Zambia 7, George Brown 8, A nuclear
bomb 9, He was the first black US senator 10, NATO

QUIZ 200

QUESTIONS FROM THE SIXTIES

1 Of which state was Marshal Voroshilov head of state in 1960?

2 Which African dam was opened in 1960 by the Queen Mother?

3 On which river was it built?

4 What was a Sunday sporting "first" in Britain in 1960?

5 Which pop singer said goodbye to the US Army in 1960?

6 What was the U-2?

7 What happened to Gary Powers' U-2?

8 Which singing duo told little Susie to wake up?

9 Which classic British car make ceased production in 1960?

10 At what did Patterson beat Johansson?

ANSWERS

1, Soviet Union 2, Kariba Dam 3, Zambezi 4, Professional soccer 5, Elvis Presley 6, A US spy plane 7, It was shot down by Soviet air defences 8, The Everly Brothers 9, Armstrong Siddeley 10, Boxing (Floyd Patterson beat Ingemar Johansson for the world heavyweight title)

QUIZ 201
QUESTIONS FROM THE SIXTIES

1. Which racing driver won the 1960 Monaco Grand Prix, and lost his driving licence the same year?

2. Which African state was hit by a disastrous earthquake in 1960?

3. Which short-lived American mail service was remembered in 1960, its 200th anniversary?

4. Which American politician spoke of a "New Frontier"?

5. Who captained the Wolverhampton Wanderers team that won the FA Cup?

6. Where were the TT races held?

7. What appeared for the first time at the May Day parade in Moscow?

8. Which mountain did the Chinese claim to have climbed by the north face?

9. Which visiting statesman told journalists he was "off on a pub crawl"?

10. In which city was he?

ANSWERS

1, Stirling Moss 2, Morocco 3, The Pony Express 4, John F Kennedy 5, Bill Slater 6, The Isle of Man 7, Missiles 8, Everest 9, Harold Macmillan 10, Paris

QUIZ 202
QUESTIONS FROM THE SIXTIES

1 What was the 1964 Fastback project designed to produce?

2 How many people watched the Apollo Moon landing on TV in 1969?

3 Which Canadian tried to buy The Times newspaper?

4 Which was the first BBC local radio station?

5 What year did it open?

6 Which Welsh town became a city in 1969?

7 In which city did Jack Ruby die in 1967?

8 Who was killed on Coniston Water in 1967?

9 What was he doing?

10 What did Stamford Brook Tube station in London have in 1964 that was unique?

ANSWERS

1, A new breed of pig 2, 600 million 3, Lord Roy Thompson of Fleet (in 1966) 4, Radio Leicester 5, 1967 6, Swansea 7, Dallas 8, Donald Campbell 9, Trying to break his own water speed record 10, London's first automatic ticket barrier

QUIZ 203

QUESTIONS FROM THE SIXTIES

1 Which mild-mannered horror-film actor died in 1969?

2 Which was the first British newspaper to issue a colour supplement?

3 When?

4 Which mountain's north face was climbed in winter for the first time in 1962?

5 Which Sunday newspaper appeared for the first time in 1962?

6 Where were the 1968 Winter Olympics held?

7 Which new arena opened in New York City in 1968?

8 On which planet did the Russians land a probe in 1966?

9 What sport did Wilt Chamberlain play?

10 What record did he achieve in 1960?

ANSWERS

1, Boris Karloff 2, The Sunday Times 3, Feb 62 4, The Matterhorn 5, The Sunday Telegraph 6, Grenoble, France 7, The new Madison Square Garden 8, Venus 9, Basketball 10, He scored all his team's 100 points, playing for Philadelphia

QUIZ 204
QUESTIONS FROM THE SIXTIES

1 Which famous US prison closed in 1963?

2 Where was it?

3 Actor Peter Lorre died in 1964; where was he born?

4 What did the D in Dwight D Eisenhower stand for?

5 What year did Eisenhower die?

6 How did the authorities get rid of the wrecked tanker "Torrey Canyon"?

7 What year was the "Torrey Canyon" disaster?

8 How many new boroughs were there in the new Greater London Council?

9 What was unusual about some London Tube trains in 1964?

10 Which country launched a satellite called "Early Bird"?

ANSWERS

1, Alcatraz 2, San Francisco Bay, California 3, Hungary 4, David 5, 1969 6, It was bombed 7, 1967 8, 32 plus the City of London 9, They had no drivers 10, The USA

QUIZ 205
QUESTIONS FROM THE SIXTIES

1 What post did Sir Edward Compton take in 1967?

2 Which new capital city was inaugurated in 1960?

3 Where were the first "open" tennis championships held in Britain?

4 Which lone sailor came home from a round-the-world voyage in April 1969?

5 Can you name his yacht?

6 What day was celebrated on 23 April throughout the 60s?

7 Which new coins first appeared in 1968?

8 Which Russian cosmonaut died in 1967 during re-entry?

9 Which US submarine stayed submerged for three months in 1960?

10 Which recently opened seaway could ships use in North America?

ANSWERS

1, Britain's first Ombudsman 2, Brasilia 3, Bournemouth 4, Robin Knox-Johnston 5, "Suhail"i 6, St George's Day! 7, 5p and 10p decimal coins 8, Vladimir Komarov 9, USS "Triton" 10, The St Lawrence Seaway (opened April 1959)

QUIZ 206
QUESTIONS FROM THE SIXTIES

1 Which new path for walkers opened in 1965 in Britain?

2 Whom did Jimmy Ellis beat to win the world heavyweight boxing title in 1968?

3 Why had Muhammad Ali had the title taken away in 1967?

4 The first woman to sit in the House of Commons died in 1964; who was she?

5 Who rode in "Freedom 7"?

6 Where did Princess Margaret get married in 1960?

7 What ran for the last time in London in 1962?

8 The star of High Noon, he died in 1961. Who was he?

9 To whom was a memorial opened at Runnymede in 1965?

10 Which group of workers were on strike in Britain in 1966, for the first time since 1911?

ANSWERS

1, The Pennine Way 2, Jerry Quarry 3, Because he refused to serve in the US military 4, Nancy, Lady Astor 5, Alan Shepard, the first American in space 6, Westminster Abbey 7, Trolleybuses 8, Gary Cooper 9, President John Kennedy 10, Seamen

QUIZ 207
QUESTIONS FROM THE SIXTIES

1 Which show closed after a record-breaking run at London's Victoria Palace Theatre?

2 How long had Coventry's new cathedral taken to build?

3 Who was its architect?

4 Where was soccer's 1967 European Cup Final played?

5 Where did Sharks and Jets meet on screen?

6 What kind of shop did Brian Epstein run before he managed the Beatles?

7 In which book does Captain Yossarian appear?

8 What did British Guiana become in 1966?

9 Zola Budd, later a controversial athlete, was born in 1966 – in which country?

10 What was different about horse racing starts in Britain after 1965?

ANSWERS

1, The Black and White Minstrel Show 2, Six years 3, Sir Basil Spence
4, Lisbon 5, In the film of West Side Story 6, A record shop 7, Catch 22
8, Guyana 9, South Africa 10, Starting stalls were introduced

QUIZ 208

QUESTIONS FROM THE SIXTIES

1 What did Nan Winton do for the first time on British TV in 1960?

2 How was "Britannia" propelled across the Atlantic in 1969?

3 What ran between Wallasey and Rhyl for the first time in 1962?

4 Which screen actor famous for his role as Sherlock Holmes died in 1967?

5 Which river was spanned by the Runcorn Bridge in 1961?

6 From whom did the Maldive Islands gain independence in 1965?

7 In which ocean are they?

8 Who made his last appearance in the House of Commons in 1964?

9 What happened to Britain's steel industry in 1967?

10 What first did Michael Darbellay of Switzerland achieve in 1963?

ANSWERS

1, Read the news 2, By oars 3, A hovercraft service 4, Basil Rathbone
5, The Mersey 6, Britain 7, Indian Ocean 8, Sir Winston Churchill 9, It was
renationalized 10, First solo ascent of the north wall of the Eiger

QUIZ 209
QUESTIONS FROM THE SIXTIES

1 Where was the liner "QE2" launched?

2 Which student quiz show began in September 1962 on British TV?

3 Who was the presenter?

4 Which oil company found oil beneath the North Sea in 1965?

5 Which liner returned to Southampton for the last time in 1967?

6 Which country launched a satellite called Alouette?

7 What was Botswana called before independence in 1966?

8 What year did Nigeria become a republic?

9 Who was left on his own in Spandau prison after October 1966?

10 Who was the first pope to visit New York?

ANSWERS

1, Clydebank, Scotland 2, University Challenge 3, Bamber Gascoigne
4, British Petroleum 5, "Queen Mary" 6, Canada 7, Bechuanaland 8, 1963
9, Rudolf Hess 10, Paul VI

QUIZ 210

QUESTIONS FROM THE SIXTIES

1 Which one of the Marx brothers played the piano?

2 What nationality was Edith Piaf?

3 What did she regret, according to her most famous song?

4 Which London railway station reopened in 1968 minus its famous arch?

5 What year did Cole Porter die?

6 What kind of business was founded by Elizabeth Arden?

7 Which member of the Crazy Gang died in October 1968?

8 To which TV series did this comedian provide the opening song?

9 Who was his stage partner?

10 Which future England soccer coach won his first cap as a player in 1964?

ANSWERS

1, Chico (who died in 1961) 2, French 3, Nothing 4, Euston 5, 1964
6, Cosmetics 7, Bud Flanagan 8, Dads' Army 9, Chesney Allen 10, Terry
Venables

QUIZ 211
QUESTIONS FROM THE SIXTIES

1 What did RSG mean for British teenager TV viewers ?

2 Who was the show's girl presenter?

3 Who was "the Shrimp"?

4 Who starred in The Cincinnatti Kid?

5 Which Russian writer, author of Quiet Flows the Don won a Nobel prize in 1965?

6 Which animal escaped for the second time from London Zoo in December 1965?

7 What was stolen and later found in a garden by a dog named Pickles?

8 Where was Chi-Chi bound in the spring of 1966?

9 What was the object of this meeting?

10 Of what did Leslie O'Brien become governor in 1966?

ANSWERS

1, Ready Steady Go 2, Cathy McGowan 3, Model Jean Shrimpton 4, Steve McQueen 5, Mikhail Sholokhov 6, Goldie the eagle 7, The World Cup 8, To meet An-An, a male giant panda 9, To produce a giant panda cub in captivity (it did not succeed) 10, The Bank of England

QUIZ 212

QUESTIONS FROM THE SIXTIES

1. What did Shell find off Great Yarmouth in 1966?
2. Which horse won the Gold Cup for the third year running in 1966?
3. Which party won the 1966 British general election?
4. Who handed over power to Suharto?
5. And where was this?
6. What went up with a bang in Dublin?
7. Which writer, who died in 1966, refused to watch television?
8. Where did a British airliner crash in Japan in March 1966?
9. What were a British doctor's average earnings in the mid 60s?
10. Whose Lola failed in Indianapolis?

ANSWERS

1, Oil 2, Arkle 3, Labour 4, Sukarno 5, Indonesia 6, Nelson's Column 7, Evelyn Waugh 8, On Mount Fuji 9, About £4000 10, Jackie Stewart's (he had to drop out when leading the Indy 500 in 1966)

QUIZ 213

QUESTIONS FROM THE SIXTIES

1 Of which kingdom did Faisal become ruler in November 1964?

2 What title was given to Princess Margaret's son, born in 1961?

3 Who was Tatum O'Neal's actor father?

4 Who was George Walker's boxing brother?

5 Which Romanian gymnast was born in November 1961?

6 What was Surtsey?

7 And where did it appear in 1963?

8 Which famous father died in November 1969?

9 Which road tunnel eased cross-Thames traffic in 1963?

10 Which soccer player scored his 1000th goal in 1969?

ANSWERS

1, Saudi Arabia 2, Viscount Linley 3, Ryan O'Neal 4, Billy 5, Nadia Comaneci
6, A volcanic island 7, It came out of the sea off Iceland 8, Joseph Kennedy
9, The Dartford Tunnel 10, Pele

QUIZ 216
QUESTIONS FROM THE SIXTIES

1 In which series did Jeff Tracy's five sons star?

2 What were the five names?

3 After whom were they named?

4 What did 1960 TV ads tell people to go to work on?

5 From which Beatles album did Michelle come?

6 Which group recorded it and reached number one in 1966?

7 Which town did the Troggs come from?

8 Under what name did Mary O'Brien sing her way to the top?

9 Can you name her first hit single?

10 How many nervous breakdowns are there in a famous 1966 Rolling Stones song title?

ANSWERS

1, Thunderbirds 2, Scott, Virgil, Alan, Gordon and John? 3, The first US astronauts 4, An egg 5, Rubber Soul 6, The Overlanders 7, Andover 8, Dusty Springfield 9, I Only Want To Be With You 10, Nineteen

QUIZ 217
QUESTIONS FROM THE SIXTIES

1 Who sang "Yellow Submarine" on the Beatles' track?

2 Brian and Carl Wilson were two of the ....?

3 Which group hit the top in 1967 with I'm A Believer?

4 Who wrote this song?

5 Who was the only non-American Monkee?

6 What was the theme song from the 1967 film Countess of Hong Kong?

7 Who wrote it?

8 Who sang it in four languages?

9 What were the languages?

10 What name did Gerry Dorsey adopt?

ANSWERS

1, Ringo Starr 2, Beach Boys 3, The Monkees 4, Neil Diamond 5, Davy Jones 6, This Is My Song 7, Charlie Chaplin 8, Petula Clark 9, French, Italian, German and (lastly) English 10, Engelbert Humperdinck

QUIZ 218
QUESTIONS FROM THE SIXTIES

1　Who made a TV film called The Magical Mystery Tour?

2　Who took over from Paul Jones as Manfred Mann's lead singer?

3　Who backed Wayne Fontana?

4　Where did windsurfing first catch on?

5　Was it an American invention?

6　Had Scrabble been invented in 1960?

7　How about Trivial Pursuit?

8　Whose boyfriend was Ken in 1961?

9　How long had Lego been on sale in 1960?

10　Who wrote about Adam Dalgleish?

ANSWERS

1, The Beatles 2, Mike D'Abo 3, The Mindbenders 4, The United States
5, Possibly not; one claim is that it was first done in Britain in 1958 6, Yes
(1948) 7, No (1981) 8, Barbie 9, Five years 10, P D James

QUIZ 219

QUESTIONS FROM THE SEVENTIES

1 Who recorded a 1976 album called Children of the World?

2 Which long running soap opera screened its 1000th episode in August, 1970?

3 By what method was convicted double murderer Gary Gilmore executed?

4 Up Around the Bend was a 1970 hit for which group?

5 Mother Teresa, the Nobel Peace Prize winner of 1979, was born in which country?

6 Which band followed Figaro in 1978 with a song called Beautiful Lover?

7 The first woman to climb Mount Everest, Junko Tabei, was from which country?

8 Which Hollywood legend was paid $2 million for his cameo appearance in Superman?

9 What did Michael Angelow do at Lord's, setting a precedent?

10 After a run of bad results in 1975 the Soviet national football team were replaced by which club side?

ANSWERS

1, The Bee Gees 2, Coronation Street 3, He was shot by a five-man firing squad 4, Creedence Clearwater Revival 5, Albania (now Macedonia) 6, Brotherhood of Man 7, Japan 8, Marlon Brando 9, He was the first streaker at a Test match in England 10, Dynamo Kiev

QUIZ 220
QUESTIONS FROM THE SEVENTIES

1 What was Alan Hudson's sport?

2 Who was the first boxer to beat Muhammad Ali in a world title fight?

3 Which forms did people in the UK love to fill in in 1971?

4 What was withdrawn from schools in 1971?

5 Who wrote The Exorcist?

6 Who played the film role of a girl possessed by the Devil?

7 Who said he'd tax the rich until the pips squeak?

8 Who opened Sydney's opera home in 1973?

9 Where did Rauf Denktash lead a separatist movement?

10 What art did Dame Barbara Hepworth practice?

ANSWERS

1 Soccer 2, Joe Frazier 3, Census forms 4, Free milk 5, William Blatty
6, Linda Blair 7, Denis Healey 8, The Queen 9, Turkish part of Cyprus
10, Sculpture

QUIZ 221
QUESTIONS FROM THE SEVENTIES

1 Who sang Bright Eyes in 1979?

2 What animals featured in the film from which it came?

3 What was the film's title?

4 Which schoolteacher became the focus of anti-police protests after his death at a rally?

5 Which country did an Israeli premier visit for the first time in 1979?

6 Of which country, did Bishop Muzorewa became prime minister in 1979?

7 Where do passengers ride the Jubilee Line?

8 In which TV show did Maureen Lipman play an agony aunt?

9 What was Kelly Monteith's native country?

10 Was he a singer, a comedian or a weatherman?

ANSWERS

1, Art Garfunkel 2, Rabbits 3, Watership Down 4, Blair Peach 5, Egypt
6, Rhodesia 7, London 8, Agony 9, Canada 10, A comedian

QUIZ 222

QUESTIONS FROM THE SEVENTIES

1   What did Snow Knight win in 1974?

2   What happened at Flixborough that year?

3   What was Tony Greig's sport?

4   What post did Jacques Chirac take up in 1974?

5   Who was Donald Coggan?

6   Which lord disappeared from home in 1974?

7   With which London gambling club was he linked?

8   What was this lord's nickname?

9   Of what crime was he suspected?

10 Who played Roy Neary in a film about aliens?

ANSWERS

1, The Derby 2, A chemical plant explosion killed 29 people 3, Cricket
4, French premier 5, Archbichop of Canterbury (1974) 6, Lord Lucan 7, The
Clermont 8, Lucky 9, Murdering the family nanny (in mistake for his wife)
10, Richard Dreyfuss

QUIZ 223
QUESTIONS FROM THE SEVENTIES

1 What was the Beatles last single?

2 Who had a US number one with War?

3 In which country was racing driver Jochen Rindt killed?

4 Of which country was Salazar (died 1970) dictator?

5 Whose London grave was vandalized in 1970?

6 Where was it?

7 Who beat Jose Manuel Ibar to win a European title?

8 How old was the Queen Mother in 1970?

9 Who wrote the music for Jesus Christ Superstar?

10 Who wrote the lyrics?

ANSWERS

1, Let It Be (1970) 2, Edwin Starr 3, Italy 4, Portugal 5, Karl Marx
6, Highgate Cemetery 7, Henry Cooper 8, 70 9, Andrew Lloyd Webber
10, Tim Rice 11, Oh Calcutta!

QUIZ 224
QUESTIONS FROM THE SEVENTIES

1 Who played a gangster called Devlin in *Performance*?

2 Who wrote the book on which the film *The Andromeda Strain* was based?

3 Which prime minister's wife published a book of poems in 1970?

4 What did Allen Lane (died 1970) do?

5 Which church decided yes to women ministers?

6 Who played a centenarian Indian in *Little Big Man*?

7 Who sang the title song to the *Aristocats*?

8 Which film told the story of Pearl Harbor?

9 Which famous racehorse died in 1970?

10 Where was Mrs Bandaranaike prime minister?

ANSWERS

1, James Fox 2, Michael Crichton 3, Mary Wilson 4, Published the first Penguin Books 5, Methodists 6, Dustin Hoffman 7, Maurice Chevalier 8, Tora! Tora! Tora! 9, Arkle 10, Ceylon (Sri Lanka)

QUIZ 225

QUESTIONS FROM THE SEVENTIES

1 What fell on Scarborough in 1975?

2 What extra facial feature did Prince Charles grow?

3 Which Commonwealth country was he visiting at the time?

4 Who was chosen to lead the Conservative Party in 1975?

5 At which tube station in London did 35 people die in a crash?

6 Which US singer performed Laughter in the Rain?

7 Which famous West Indies cricketer was knighted in 1975?

8 What was the score in the 1975 FA Cup Final

9 Who beat whom in this game?

10 Which team was Bobby Moore playing for in the match?

ANSWERS

1, A meteorite 2, A beard 3, Canada 4, Margaret Thatcher 5, Moorgate
6, Neil Sedaka 7, Gary Sobers 8, 2-0 9, West Ham beat Fulham 10, Fulham

QUIZ 226

QUESTIONS FROM THE SEVENTIES

1 Which British city was hit by IRA bombs in November 1974?

2 Where did Karamanlis become president?

3 Which former Secretary General of the United Nations died in 1974?

4 For which English club did Martin Buchan play soccer?

5 Which newspaper stopped its Saturday edition in 1974?

6 Which country cancelled plans to build a high speed train?

7 Which group sang Seven Seas of Rhye?

8 In which year did Wales not finish either first or second in the Five Nations rugby championship?

9 Which Australian city was damaged by a cyclone?

10 Which British MP disappeared from a beach in Miami?

ANSWERS

1, Birmingham 2, Greece 3, U Thant 4, Manchester United 5, The Evening Standard (London) 6, Britain 7, Queen 8, 1972 9, Darwin 10, John Stonehouse

QUIZ 227

QUESTIONS FROM THE SEVENTIES

1 What landed 362 passengers at Heathrow for the first time in January 1970?

2 Who was fined £200 for possession of cannabis in 1970?

3 Where did the 1970 winter 'flu outbreak come from?

4 What was happening in Mexico in 1970?

5 What event did Gay Trip win in 1970?

6 Which famous British philosopher died in February 1970?

7 Who acted as A Question of Sport's first quizmaster?

8 In what TV programme did Frankie Howerd play a Roman slave?

9 Who were Tim, Graeme and Bill?

10 What were their full names?

ANSWERS

1, A Boeing 747 (jumbo jet) 2, Mick Jagger 3, Hong Kong 4, The World Cup
5, The Grand National 6, Bertrand Russell 7, David Vine 8, Up Pompeii
9, The Goodies 10, Tim Brooke Taylor, Graeme Garden, Bill Oddie

QUIZ 228
QUESTIONS FROM THE SEVENTIES

1 Who played Mr Abbott in Bless This House?

2 Which Peter starred in The Onedin Line?

3 Who sang One Bad Apple in 1971?

4 What happened on 15th February 1971?

5 Which African country did Princess Anne visit in 1970?

6 In which country did Milton Obote lose his job?

7 In which European country did people riot in 1970 over food prices?

8 Which 1970s glamour competition was disrupted by demonstrators?

9 In which country did 146 people die in a 1970 dance hall fire?

10 For whom did Felix play soccer in 1970?

ANSWERS

1, Sid James 2, Peter Gilmore 3, The Osmonds 4, Decimalization 5, Kenya
6, Uganda 7, Poland 8, Miss World 9, France 10, Brazil

QUIZ 229
QUESTIONS FROM THE SEVENTIES

1 Who were the Bellamys?

2 Who married Margaret Sinclair?

3 Who made an album called Pictures at an Exhibition?

4 Where was President Levington deposed?

5 Whose Hot Love reached number 1 in 1971?

6 Who sang Gypsies, Tramps and Thieves?

7 Where in Europe did women get the right to vote in 1971?

8 Where was Erich Honecker the man in charge?

9 Who married a beauty called Bianca in 1971?

10 Who led British negotiations with the EEC?

ANSWERS

1, The Upstairs family in Upstairs Downstairs 2, Pierre Trudeau 3, Emerson, Lake and Palmer 4, Argentina 5, T Rex 6, Cher 7, Switzerland 8, East Germany 9, Mick Jagger 10, Geoffrey Rippon

QUIZ 230
QUESTIONS FROM THE SEVENTIES

1　Where was Papa Doc president?

2　Who took over from him when he died in 1971?

3　And his nickname was?

4　How did the Daily Mail change in 1971?

5　Who sang Joy to the World?

6　What was new about a trip to the Natural History Museum in 1971?

7　Where was the Mariner 9 spacecraft sent to?

8　Which English soccer team did the double in 1971?

9　Who came second to this team in the League?

10　And which team did they beat in the FA Cup Final?

ANSWERS

1, Haiti 2, His son 3, Baby Doc 4, It went tabloid 5, Three Dog Night
6, Museum charges were introduced 7, Mars 8, Arsenal 9, Leeds
10, Liverpool

QUIZ 231
QUESTIONS FROM THE SEVENTIES

1 Where did Charles Haughey become prime minister?

2 Which Asian country did the USSR invade in 1979?

3 Which group sang Babe?

4 Why was the Shah on the move in 1979?

5 Where did he eventually find a refuge?

6 Who won the 1979 Nobel Peace Prize?

7 In which city did she do her work?

8 In which country was she born?

9 Which group had a hit with Another Brick in the Wall?

10 Who won the US Open Golf title for the first time in 1979?

ANSWERS

1, Republic of Ireland 2, Afghanistan 3, Styx 4, He had been deposed in Iran 5, Panama 6, Mother Teresa 7, Calcutta 8, Albania 9, Pink Floyd 10, Fuzzy Zoeller

QUIZ 232
QUESTIONS FROM THE SEVENTIES

1 Where was Charles Lockwood captured in 1973?

2 Which part of the Skylab station was damaged and had to be repaired?

3 Who sang Can the Can?

4 Where was President Makarios re-elected?

5 Who topped the US charts with My Love in 1973?

6 Where did Fianna Fail fail in an election?

7 Which Rugby League team won the 1973 Challenge Cup Final?

8 Which Second Division soccer team won the FA Cup?

9 Which country had VAT for the first time in 1973?

10 Where did a government announce plans to save the tiger?

ANSWERS

1, Argentina 2, Solar panels 3, Suzi Quatro 4, Cyprus 5, Paul McCartney and Wings 6, Republic of Ireland (General Election 1973) 7, St Helens 8, Sunderland 9, United Kingdom 10, India

QUIZ 233

QUESTIONS FROM THE SEVENTIES

1 What did the Americans say they'd found in their Moscow embassy?

2 From which musical came the song You're the One that I Want?

3 Who played Sandy in this film?

4 With which politician did newspapers link Norman Scott?

5 Who or what was Shirley Heights?

6 In which European country was the president forced to resign in 1978?

7 Where did a gas tanker explosion kill 188 holidaymakers?

8 Which jailed leader celebrated his 60th birthday in 1978?

9 In which country were the 1978 Commonwealth Games held?

10 Which holy relic went on show in Italy?

ANSWERS

1, Bugs (listening devices) 2, Grease 3, Olivia Newton-John 4, Jeremy Thorpe 5, The 1978 Derby winner 6, Italy 7, Spain 8, Nelson Mandela 9, Canada 10, The Turin Shroud

QUIZ 234
QUESTIONS FROM THE SEVENTIES

1 In which continent did the Ogaden War take place?

2 Who lost it?

3 Who was world snooker champion in 1978?

4 Who played his first Test for England as a batsman?

5 In which English town was the sitcom Fawlty Towers supposedly set?

6 Which insurance company planned a new, hi-tech, London headquarters?

7 Who released an album called The Kick Inside?

8 Who was captain of Argentina's World Cup winning team?

9 What did Lucius do in 1978?

10 In which country were Peabody awards given to TV shows?

ANSWERS

1, Africa 2, Somalia 3, Ray Reardon 4, David Gower 5, Torquay 6, Lloyd's of London 7, Kate Bush 8, Daniela Pasarella 9, Won the Grand National 10, USA

QUIZ 235

QUESTIONS FROM THE SEVENTIES

1 What year was the voting age in the United States lowered from 21 to 18?

2 In which country did General Zhia oust Prime Minister Bhutto in 1977?

3 The German director of the influential Metropolis died in 1976. Who was he?

4 Who held office for only 33 days in 1978?

5 900 people died in a mass suicide in Guyana in 1978. Who led this bizarre cult?

6 What year was Britain's winter of discontent?

7 Which former World War II commander and member of Britain's royal family was murdered by the IRA in 1979?

8 In which country were 100 US embassy staff held hostage in 1979?

9 Which country invaded Afghanistan in 1979?

10 Who was the second husband of crime writer Agatha Christie, who died in 1976 still best known by her first husband's name?

ANSWERS

1, 1971 2, Pakistan 3, Fritz Lang 4, Pope John Paul I 5, Rev. Jim Jones
6, 1978–79 7, Earl Mountbatten of Burma 8, Iran 9, The USSR 10, Sir Max Mallowan

QUIZ 236
QUESTIONS FROM THE SEVENTIES

1 Which country's leader in 1970 was Edward Gierek?

2 James Callaghan lost his vote of confidence in 1979 by how many votes?

3 At what age could people in Britain vote after 1970?

4 Which tiny European state refused to allow women the vote in February 1971?

5 Which British politician was killed by an IRA bomb in the House of Commons car park in 1979?

6 Which European country legalized divorce in November 1970?

7 Which square in Paris was known as the Place de l'Etoile before 1970?

8 Where was the Ho Chi Minh Trail?

9 Which US university was the scene of a terrible 1970 shooting?

10 In which African country was the Biafran war, which ended in 1970?

ANSWERS

1, Poland 2, One 3, 18 4, Liechtenstein 5, Airey Neave 6, Italy 7, Place Charles De Gaulle 8, Vietnam 9, Kent State, Ohio 10, Nigeria

QUIZ 237
QUESTIONS FROM THE SEVENTIES

1 Which British daily newspaper closed down in March 1971?

2 Of which country was General Yakubu Gowon head of state?

3 Who became Argentina's president in 1973?

4 Which musical was made about his wife?

5 Of which country was Margrethe II queen?

6 Which country's prime minister was Gough Whitlam?

7 What year did East and West Germany join the United Nations?

8 Which European country was ruled by the generals in 1973?

9 Who was this country's exiled king?

10 Which island was led by Dom Mintoff?

ANSWERS

1, The Daily Sketch 2, Nigeria 3, Juan Peron 4, Evita 5, Denmark 6, Australia
7, 1973 8, Greece 9, Constantine 10, Malta

QUIZ 238
QUESTIONS FROM THE SEVENTIES

1. How many people were unemployed in Britain in 1971: 800,000, 1.8 million, or 3 million?

2. How many engines did the new TriStar and DC-10 airliners each have?

3. From where did Luna 16 return in September 1970?

4. Which Pacific ex-colony became independent in 1970?

5. A British government minister in the 90s; in 1974 a guest on the Morecambe and Wise television show. Who is she?

6. Were members of OPEC concerned about the price of oil, oranges or olives?

7. Was Bishop Muzorewa a leading figure in: a) the Rhodesia crisis or
   b) the US Civil Rights movement?

8. In which country did Kerry Packer build a media empire?

9. Who said in 1974 … "Those who hate you don't win unless you hate them"?

10. Who succeeded Richard Nixon as US President on 9 August 1974?

ANSWERS

1, 800,000 2, Three 3, The Moon 4, Fiji 5, Glenda Jackson 6, Oil 7, a)
8, Australia 9, Richard Nixon 10, Gerald R. Ford

QUIZ 239

QUESTIONS FROM THE SEVENTIES

1   Did the population of London rise or fall between 1961 and 1971?

2   What did the initials ZANU stand for in African politics?

3   What post did Sir Arthur Bliss hold from 1953 to 1975?

4   In which sport was Douglas Haston celebrated throughout the 70s?

5   Which US President did Prince Charles go to visit in July 1970?

6   Which British prime minister's wife became famous for her poems?

7   What year were the British people asked to vote whether or not to stay in the European Community?

8   David Bedford set a world record for track and field in 1973; at what distance?

9   What were first seen on British motorways in 1970?

10   What was Black Arrow?

ANSWERS

1, It fell, from 7.9 million to just under 7.4 million 2, Zimbabwe African National Union 3, Master of the Queen's Music 4, Mountain climbing 5, Richard Nixon 6, Harold Wilson's wife Mary 7, 1975 8, 10,000 metres 9, Crash barriers 10, A rocket

QUIZ 240

QUESTIONS FROM THE SEVENTIES

1 Natalia Makarova defected to the West from the USSR; was she a dancer, an athlete or a scientist?

2 In which country did Idi Amin become president in 1971?

3 Of which part of the United Kingdom was Brian Faulkner a prominent leader in the early 70s?

4 Which member of Britain's royal family died in Paris in 1972?

5 Who was convicted in 1971 for the murder of Sharon Tate and four others in Hollywood?

6 Who succeeded Harold Wilson as Britain's prime minister in 1976?

7 Who became Roman Catholic archbishop of Westminster in 1976?

8 Who left British politics in 1976 to become President of the EEC Commission?

9 Was Dame Janet Baker celebrated for her singing, cooking or scientific achievements?

10 What African country was led until 1971 by Milton Obote?

ANSWERS

1, A dancer 2, Uganda 3, Northern Ireland 4, The Duke of Windsor
5, Charles Manson 6, James Callaghan 7, Basil Hume 8, Roy Jenkins
9, Singing 10, Uganda

QUIZ 241
QUESTIONS FROM THE SEVENTIES

1 What were the first names of President Nixon's two daughters?

2 What award did Henry Kissinger accept in 1973 for the Vietnam War ceasefire?

3 Which famous Soviet scientist won worldwide admiration and the 1975 Nobel peace prize for promoting peace?

4 Which two Middle Eastern leaders shared the 1978 Nobel Peace prize?

5 Which country did Haille Selassie lead until being deposed in 1974?

6 Where did John Marshall succeed Keith Holyoake as prime minister in 1972?

7 Where did Birendra become king in 1972?

8 What post did Joseph Luns of the Netherlands accept in 1971?

9 What was Colonel Rudolf Abel who died in Moscow in 1971 known to be?

10 What British government post did David Owen take on in 1977?

ANSWERS

1, Julie and Patricia 2, Nobel peace prize 3, Andrei Sakharov 4, Menachem Begin of Israel and Anwar el-Sadat of Egypt 5, Ethiopia 6, New Zealand 7, Nepal 8, Secretary-General of NATO 9, A spy 10, Foreign Secretary

QUIZ 242
QUESTIONS FROM THE SEVENTIES

1   Of which country was Sean Lemass (died 1971) a former leader?

2   Who became famous for mysteriously bending spoons?

3   A government minister who died in 1974 left some controversial Diaries. Who was he?

4   Famous for his clock-hanging sequence and other silent film comic-heroics, he died in 1971; who was he?

5   Which South African golfer won his third British Open title in 1974?

6   Which England football manager resigned in 1977 to go to the United Arab Emirates?

7   Of which club side was he manager before becoming England boss?

8   A French actor, known for his suave style and tilted straw hats, died in 1974. Name?

9   Which famous musical duke died in 1974?

10 This President of the United States took over from Franklin D Roosevelt; he died in 1972. Who was he?

ANSWERS

1, The Irish Republic 2, Uri Geller 3, Richard Crossman 4, Harold Lloyd
5, Gary Player 6, Don Revie 7, Leeds United 8, Maurice Chevalier
9, Bandleader Duke Ellington 10, Harry S Truman

QUIZ 243

QUESTIONS FROM THE SEVENTIES

1 To whom did George Foreman lose the big fight of 1974?

2 For what was John McVicar notorious in Britain in 1970?

3 Salford's most famous painter died in 1976; who was he?

4 The man recognized as the father of the BBC died in 1971. Who was he?

5 Which formidable dame of the stage exited in 1976?

6 Which composer known for his work with the singer Peter Pears died in 1976?

7 What nationality was the comedian Fernandel, who died in 1971?

8 Which once-divine Asian head of state visited Britain in 1971?

9 The wife of one of the Allied leaders in World War II died in 1977; who was she?

10 Which England footballer left Liverpool for Hamburg in 1977?

ANSWERS

1, Muhammad Ali 2, Escaping from prison 3, L S Lowry 4, Lord Reith
5, Edith Evans 6, Benjamin Britten 7, French 8, Emperor Hirohito of Japan
9, Lady Spencer Churchill (widow of Sir Winston Churchill) 10, Kevin
Keegan

QUIZ 244

QUESTIONS FROM THE SEVENTIES

1 Of which country was Pierre Trudeau prime minister during the 70s?

2 Egypt's president died in 1970. Who was he?

3 Which famous Frenchman died in November 1970?

4 Which famous British racing driver died in 1975?

5 Which country was ruled by Papa Doc Duvalier?

6 Bebe Daniels died in 1971; what was the name of husband and showbiz partner?

7 What was Gypsy Rose Lee (died 1970) famous for?

8 This leader once took off his shoe to bang the rostrum at the UN; he died in 1971. Who was he?

9 Whose lordly disappearance in 1974 sparked a man-hunt?

10 Why were the police seeking this person?

ANSWERS

1, Canada 2, Nasser 3, Charles De Gaulle 4, Graham Hill 5, Haiti 6, Ben Lyon 7, Stripping 8, Nikita Khruschev 9, Lord Lucan 10, He was suspected of murdering his child's nanny in London

QUIZ 245
QUESTIONS FROM THE SEVENTIES

1 He made Stagecoach and many other Westerns, and died in 1973. Who was he?

2 Veronica Lake who died in 1973 was a famous: a) model b) singer or c) film actress?

3 For what was John Cranko (died 1973) famous?

4 He starred in The Cruel Sea and died in 1973; who was he?

5 For what was David Lack (died 1973) best known?

6 She wrote Love in a Cold Climate and died in 1973; her name?

7 Star of horror films, son of a famous father; died 1973. Name?

8 What instrument did jazzman Tubby Hayes (died 1973) play?

9 Louis Saint Laurent, who died in 1973, led which Commonwealth country?

10 Who was the Flying Finn, a runner who died in 1973?

11 Wilfred Rhodes, who died in 1973, was a famous sportsman:
a) cricketer b) soccer player or c) tennis star?

ANSWERS

1, John Ford 2, c) 3, Ballet dancer 4, Jack Hawkins 5, He was a naturalist 6, Nancy Mitford 7, Lon Chaney Jr 8, Saxophone 9, Canada 10, Paavo Nurmi

QUIZ 246
QUESTIONS FROM THE SEVENTIES

1   From which party did Lord George-Brown resign in 1976?

2   Who was the royal commander of HMS Bronington?

3   Which wartime commander, known to soldiers as Monty, died in 1976?

4   Which royal couple agreed to part in 1976?

5   She starred in many films as a dotty English lady, played Miss Marple, and died in 1971. Who was she?

6   In what sphere did Otto Klemperer win fame?

7   Abebe Bikila (died 1973) was famous as … what?

8   Was Bobby Darin (died 1973) a singer, a politician, or a baseball star?

9   What instrument did Pablo Casals play?

10 For what was Kenneth Allsop best known?

ANSWERS

1, The Labour Party 2, The Prince of Wales 3, Field Marshal Viscount Montgomery 4, Princess Margaret and Lord Snowdon 5, Margaret Rutherford 6, Orchestral conductor 7, An athlete, Ethiopia's first international running star 8, A singer 9, Cello 10, His TV broadcasts and journalism

QUIZ 247
QUESTIONS FROM THE EIGHTIES

1 What was Sizewell B?

2 Was Jim Bakker a TV evangelist, a runner under drugs suspicion or the new boss of Ford?

3 Who went walkabout in the Kalahari Desert in 1987?

4 Which TV comedy made the Resistance a joke?

5 Which tartan airline was swallowed by BA?

6 Barlow Clowes collapsed in 1988. What was it?

7 Which African state was bombed by US jets in 1986?

8 Who said 'We can do business together'?

9 And of whom?

10 Which unshaven pop star made Band Aid big news?

ANSWERS

1, A proposed new nuclear power station 2, A TV evangelist 3, Prince Charles 4, 'Allo 'Allo 5, British Caledonian 6, An investment company 7, Libya 8, Margaret Thatcher 9, Mikhail Gorbachev 10, Bob Geldof

QUIZ 248
QUESTIONS FROM THE EIGHTIES

1 Which Atlantic island was used as a staging post during the Falklands War?

2 Which Australian tycoon bought Times Newspapers in 1981?

3 Which noble assembly went on TV for the first time?

4 Do you know in which year?

5 Who won the battle to own Harrods?

6 What was the name of his beaten rival?

7 Name the North Sea oil rig which caught fire in 1988.

8 Which Victor Hugo story was a musical hit?

9 Complete the film title: Desperately Seeking -----?

10 Where was the Achille Lauro hijacked?

ANSWERS

1, Ascension Island 2, Rupert Murdoch 3, The House of Lords 4, 1985
5, Mohammed Al-Fayed 6, Lonrho boss Tiny Rowland 7, Piper Alpha
8, Les Miserables 9, Susan 10, The Mediterranean

QUIZ 249

QUESTIONS FROM THE EIGHTIES

1 Where did a group of 'Argentine scrap dealers' land in 1982?

2 What were 'SS-20's?

3 Who got married on 29 July 1981?

4 Which airline was bossed by Lord King?

5 Whose cricketing deeds at Headingley stirred English supporters?

6 Which leader was assassinated in Cairo?

7 Which musical was based on T.S. Eliot's poems?

8 Who made his first appearance as Indiana Jones in 1981?

9 What was the film called?

10 ASLEF went on strike in 1982. What was affected: a) power supplies b) trains c) schools?

ANSWERS

1, South Georgia 2, Soviet missiles 3, Prince Charles and Lady Diana Spencer 4, British Airways 5, Ian Botham 6, Anwar Sadat 7, Cats 8, Harrison Ford 9, Raiders of the Lost Ark 10, b)

QUIZ 250
QUESTIONS FROM THE EIGHTIES

1 Where was the Lenin shipyard?

2 Which nation was fighting a civil war with large Soviet forces helping the government?

3 Who made the 1981 'Limehouse Declaration'?

4 Which party did they found?

5 Who was Professor Alan Walters?

6 Which actor's Macbeth raised eyebrows?

7 What was the ASB?

8 In what year was John Lennon murdered?

9 Which London palace was damaged by fire the same year?

10 Which submarine-launched missile was the Royal Navy buying?

ANSWERS

1, Gdansk, Poland 2, Afghanistan 3, The so-called 'Gang of Four'
4, The Social Democrats 5, The UK government's adviser on monetary
policy 6, Peter O'Toole's 7, The Church of England's Alternative Service
Book 8, 1980 9, Alexandra Palace 10, Trident

QUIZ 251
QUESTIONS FROM THE EIGHTIES

1 Who succeeded Jeremy Isaacs as boss of Channel 4?

2 Who owned BPCC?

3 Which singer bowed out of Watford FC in 1987?

4 And which tycoon said he wanted to buy it?

5 What did the government announce in 1987 would be introduced on 1 April 1990?

6 Where was hostage Roger Auque freed?

7 Who said London's planners had wrecked its skyline?

8 Where were 16 white people murdered at Esigodini mission?

9 In which state was Quiryat Shemona army camp?

10 Who painted Souvenir du Havre, sold for £4 million?

ANSWERS

1, Michael Grade 2, Robert Maxwell 3, Elton John 4, Robert Maxwell
5, The poll tax 6, Beirut 7, Prince Charles 8. Zimbabwe 9, Israel
10, Picasso

QUIZ 252
QUESTIONS FROM THE EIGHTIES

1 The actor who played PC Dixon on TV died in 1981. Name?

2 Who played the minister in Yes, Minister?

3 From which port did the Falklands task force sail?

4 How was Jeffrey Bernard, according to a play title?

5 What product did coy flatmates getting friendlier famously advertise on TV?

6 Who was Sonia Sutcliffe?

7 Which city elected David Dinkins mayor?

8 Which royal couple separated in 1981?

9 Which 'red-led' council did the Conservatives abolish?

10 What engulged Bhopal?

ANSWERS

1, Jack Warner 2, Paul Eddington 3, Portsmouth 4, Unwell 5, Gold Blend coffee 6, Wife of the 'Yorkshire Ripper' 7, New York City 8, Princess Anne and Captain Mark Phillips 9, The GLC 10, A poisonous chemical cloud

QUIZ 253
QUESTIONS FROM THE EIGHTIES

1 Who sang West End Girls?

2 Once Frank Spencer on TV, now star of Phantom of the Opera. Name?

3 Which UK bank was privatised in 1986?

4 Which palace nearly burned down that year?

5 In which city were house prices rising by 25% in 1987-88?

6 Which disease killed three people at the BBC?

7 For what cause did people wear red noses?

8 Which UN boss denied he'd ever been a Nazi?

9 Which Swedish premier was murdered in 1986?

10 Which new European warplane project was launched in 1985?

ANSWERS

1, Pet Shop Boys 2, Michael Crawford 3, The TSB 4, Hampton Court
5, London 6, Legionnaires' Disease 7, Comic Relief 8, Kurt Waldheim
9, Olof Palme 10, Eurofighter

QUIZ 254
QUESTIONS FROM THE EIGHTIES

1 Was Hotel du Lac a book, a film, or a perfume?

2 Which adolescent's Secret Diary was a bestseller?

3 What was Das Boot about?

4 Which seaside town was the setting for an attempt to murder members of the Cabinet?

5 What was Mrs Thatcher's son's name?

6 Who was made Earl of Stockton?

7 Which churchman expressed doubts about the Virgin Birth?

8 Where is the Golden Temple?

9 And to which religious group was it sacred?

10 Who chose Mondale to be their man?

ANSWERS

1, A book 2, Adrian Mole's 3, A German U-boat 4, Brighton 5, Mark
6, Harold Macmillan 7, The Bishop of Durham 8, Amritsar 9, Sikhs
10, US Democrats in 1984

QUIZ 255
QUESTIONS FROM THE EIGHTIES

1 Which Japanese firm said it would build cars in Sunderland?

2 Of what was Michael Bettany found guilty in 1984?

3 Outside whose embassy was a policewoman shot in 1984?

4 What was Soviet leader Chernenko's first name?

5 Where was Terry Waite kidnapped?

6 Who called for 'glasnost'?

7 Who moved from British Steel to be boss of the NCB in 1983?

8 And what was the NCB?

9 Who lost his sprint medal after failing a 1988 drugs test?

10 Which politician got egg on her face over salmonella?

ANSWERS

1, Nissan 2, Spying 3, The Libyan Embassy in London 4, Konstantin
5, Beirut 6, Mikhail Gorbachev 7, Ian MacGregor 8, National Coal Board
9, Ben Johnson 10, Edwina Currie

QUIZ 256
QUESTIONS FROM THE EIGHTIES

1 Which actor recreated a TV role in The Return of Sam McCloud (1989)?

2 In which explorer's footsteps did Robert Swan tread?

3 And where did he and two companions reach in January 1986?

4 What seen in 1985 will reappear in 2061?

5 Who was the civil servant accused of breaching the Official Secrets Act, but acquitted in 1985?

6 In which sport was Bernhard Langer a champion?

7 What was his nationality?

8 What did Sean Kelly ride?

9 Where were Owlprowl spotters on the lookout for night fliers?

10 Which 80s year was British Film Year?

ANSWERS

1, Dennis Weaver 2, Captain Scott's 3, The South Pole 4, Halley's Comet
5, Clive Ponting 6, Golf 7, West German 8, Racing bicycles 9, London
(counting owls) 10, 1985

QUIZ 257
QUESTIONS FROM THE EIGHTIES

1 Complete the 1987 film title: Robo...?

2 In which city was The Running Man set?

3 Phil Lynott died in 1986; with which band did he play?

4 Which Police singer appeared in the film Brimstone and Treacle?

5 Complete the pop duo: Daryl Hall and ......?

6 And these pop names... The Flying P...?

7 Lloyd Cole and the ....?

8 Feargal S.....?

9 Which fashion company appeared on the Grand Prix circuit?

10 Who was the youngest-ever Northern Ireland soccer international (1982)?

ANSWERS

1, Robocop 2, Los Angeles 3, Thin Lizzy 4, Sting 5, John Oates 6, Pickets
7, Commotions 8, Sharkey 9, Benetton 10, Norman Whiteside

QUIZ 258

QUESTIONS FROM THE EIGHTIES

1 Whose 'Welcome to the Pleasure Dome' album broke records in 1984?

2 Which octogenarian sang 'I Wish I Was 18 Again'?

3 Which country was the scene of the worst-ever train disaster (1981)?

4 This country lost an airliner in 1985; over which ocean?

5 And what caused the disaster?

6 Who was Canada's most notorious runner?

7 Who scored a century and took 10 wickets in a 1980 Test for England?

8 On which ground did he do it?

9 What were stored at RAF Molesworth, amid protests?

10 What flew from London to Sydney in record time in 1985?

ANSWERS

1, Frankie Goes to Hollywood 2, George Burns 3, India 4, Atlantic
5, A terrorist bomb 6, Ben Johnson 7, Ian Botham 8, Bombay, India
9, Cruise missiles 10, Concorde

QUIZ 259

QUESTIONS FROM THE EIGHTIES

1 Which sporting hero was honoured in 1984 with a statue at Wimbledon?

2 What did Admiral Woodward command?

3 In which TV series did Gillian Taylforth appear?

4 In which TV show did the Duchess of York play silly games?

5 Which newspaper did Tiny Rowland own?

6 Whom did Robin Givens marry, and divorce?

7 Who was Sir Ralph Halpern?

8 Which US Presidential candidate saw his hopes dashed by a 'relationship' scandal?

9 Which rat became a TV star?

10 What were 'Transformers'?

ANSWERS

1, Fred Perry 2, The Falklands Task Force 3, EastEnders 4, It's A Knockout
5, The Observer 6, Mike Tyson 7, Chairman of the Burton Group
8, Gary Hart 9, Roland Rat 10, Popular action-toys

QUIZ 260
QUESTIONS FROM THE EIGHTIES

1 What was the scandal in the film Scandal?

2 In 1983 Lady Donaldson became the first female... what?

3 Who partnered Jayne on ice?

4 What country did Lee Kuan Yew lead?

5 Which boys' organization was 100 years old in 1983?

6 What did Ed Mirvish buy?

7 Which horse won the 1981 Derby?

8 In which country was it later kidnapped?

9 What was the sport in which Jarmila Kratochvilova caused controversy?

10 On what subject did the Royal College of Physicians publish an alarming report in 1983?

ANSWERS

1, The 1963 Profumo scandal 2, Lord Mayor of London 3, Christopher Dean
4, Singapore 5, The Boys' Brigade 6, The Old Vic Theatre 7, Shergar
8, Ireland 9, Athletics 10, Cigarette smoking

QUIZ 261
QUESTIONS FROM THE EIGHTIES

1 Which 1984 film took Peggy Ashcroft to India?

2 Which political party had Militant problems?

3 What went onto Londoners' wheels for the first time in 1983?

4 Who was Sally Ride?

5 Which European river was polluted by a 1986 chemical spill?

6 Where did the Marchioness disaster happen?

7 Which Boomtown Rat got an honorary knighthood?

8 Where did a 1987 heatwave kill 1000 people?

9 What hit the USS Stark in 1987?

10 What or who was Risley, in the news in 1989?

ANSWERS

1, A Passage to India 2, Labour 3, Wheel clamps 4, A US astronaut
5, The Rhine 6, River Thames in London 7, Bob Geldof 8, Greece 9, An Iraqi missile 10, A remand centre, where a riot took place

QUIZ 262
QUESTIONS FROM THE EIGHTIES

1 What did 24 Royal Marines do in mid air in 1986?

2 Who waved from the Buckingham Palace balcony that year?

3 Where was Mount Pleasant airport opened?

4 Ruled since 1945, died in 1985; who was he?

5 Who made the pop video Thriller?

6 Name Boy George's band.

7 Which European state was co-ruled by the Bishop of Urgel?

8 Which sporting team did Allan Border lead?

9 By what name was runner Mary Decker known after her marriage?

10 Whom did Gorbachev succeed as Soviet leader?

ANSWERS

1, They set a new world record for parachute 'stacking' 2, The Duke and Duchess of York 3, The Falklands 4, Enver Hoxha of Albania 5, Michael Jackson 6, Culture Club 7, Andorra 8, Australia's cricketers 9, Slaney 10, Konstantin Chernenko

QUIZ 263

QUESTIONS FROM THE EIGHTIES

1 Where was the world's tallest chimney built in 1987?

2 Who started the Today newspaper in 1986?

3 Whose C5 hummed to a standstill?

4 Who said 'the hand of God' helped him score a goal?

5 In which competition?

6 Who tripped up the American favourite in the women's 3000m in the 1984 Olympics?

7 Who was the fallen American?

8 Which England cricketer wagged his finger at an umpire?

9 Who was snooker's 'Hurricane'?

10 Which former UK prime minister died in 1987?

ANSWERS

1, Kazakhstan 2, Eddie Shah 3. Sir Clive Sinclair 4, Diego Maradona 5, The 1986 World Cup 6, Zola Budd 7, Mary Decker 8, Mike Gatting 9, Alex Higgins 10, Harold Macmillan

QUIZ 264
QUESTIONS FROM THE EIGHTIES

1 Who bought Fountains Abbey in 1983?

2 In 1986, what the average pocket money given to a child in Britain?

3 And how many people out of 100 went to the cinema every week?

4 Which actor planned to rebuild Shakespeare's Globe?

5 Which Commonwealth country ended its last legal links with Britain in 1986?

6 Which company built the most cars in the mid 80s?

7 Who became president of Austria, denying a Nazi past?

8 Which country did Samora Machel lead?

9 Which team beat Liverpool in the 1985 European Cup final?

10 28 years of defeat, and a tie, ended in 1985 - where?

ANSWERS

1, The National Trust 2, £1.17 a week 3, Two 4, Sam Wanamaker
5, Australia 6, General Motors 7, Kurt Waldheim 8, Mozambique
9, Juventus 10, The Belfry

QUIZ 265
QUESTIONS FROM THE EIGHTIES

1 What did Britain and France agree in 1986 to have open by 1993?

2 Where was 'Maya's Tomb' discovered?

3 In which US state did Prince Charles try on a cowboy hat?

4 Which film won the 1986 Oscar for best picture?

5 Which was the first British daily paper to print in colour every day?

6 Which birds were used to guard US army bases in Germany?

7 Which king was the first foreign monarch to address both Houses of Parliament?

8 Where was Expo 86 held?

9 Who opened it?

10 Which powerboat set a new trans-Atlantic record in 1986?

ANSWERS

1, The Channel Tunnel 2, Egypt 3, Texas 4, Out of Africa 5, Today 6, Geese 7, King Juan Carlos of Spain 8, Vancouver 9, The Prince and Princess of Wales 10, Virgin Atlantic Challenger II

QUIZ 266
QUESTIONS FROM THE EIGHTIES

1 What caused 1984 riots in Morocco: a) food prices b) religious conflict c) soccer rivalry?

2 Where did Bruce McCandless float free in 1984?

3 At which airport was Terminal 4 opened in 1985?

4 Where was the body of Josef Mengele exhumed?

5 And who was he?

6 Which Asian city was host to Wham! in 1985?

7 Deer from Britain were released into the native land where they had died out in the 1930s. Which deer?

8 And to which country did they return?

9 Which European country governed New Caledonia?

10 Where did Jerry Rawlings seize power in 1982?

ANSWERS

1, a) 2, In space (without a safety line) 3, Heathrow 4, Brazil
5, A Nazi war criminal who died in 1979 6, Beijing 7, Père David's deer
8, China 9, France 10, Ghana

QUIZ 267
QUESTIONS FROM THE EIGHTIES

1 Who campaigned in 1984 with the slogan 'Leadership That's Working'?

2 How successful was it?

3 What was the title of Helen Hoover Santmyer's 1984 novel?

4 How long had it taken her to write?

5 Where was she living when it became a bestseller: a) in a nursing home b) in a shack in the mountains c) in jail?

6 Which British actress's memoirs were entitled For Adults Only (she died in 1984)?

7 The inventor of the opinion poll died in 1984: who was he/she?

8 And what fast food chain had Ray Kroc founded?

9 What art forger's own paintings fetched £72,000 at auction in 1983?

10 Where was Adam Malik a leading political figure?

ANSWERS

1, Ronald Reagan 2, He won a landslide victory 3, ----And Ladies of the Club 4, Over 50 years 5, a) 6, Diana Dors 7, George Gallup 8, McDonald's 9, Tom Keating's 10, Indonesia

QUIZ 268
QUESTIONS FROM THE EIGHTIES

1 Which Disney character was 50 years old in 1984?

2 Which swimmer could do a length in just 29 strokes?

3 Which cricket team beat England 5-0 in 1984?

4 Who was the winning captain?

5 When should you never feed Gremlins (according to the film)?

6 What was the title of the 1984 Band Aid record?

7 Which RAF pilot played on the wing for England?

8 In which sport was this?

9 Who was the 3rd woman tennis player to complete the Grand Slam?

10 With whom did she complete a doubles Grand Slam?

ANSWERS

1, Donald Duck 2, Michael Gross 3, West Indies 4, Clive Lloyd
5, After midnight 6, 'Don't They Know It's Christmas'?
7, Rory Underwood 8, Rugby Union 9, Martina Navratilova 10, Pam Shriver

QUIZ 269
QUESTIONS FROM THE EIGHTIES

1 Whose 'Super Trooper' was their last chart-topper?

2 In which sport was Australia's Richard Charlesworth a veteran star?

3 Who claimed a record 356th Test wicket in 1986?

4 What kind of animal was baby Le Le?

5 What was the USAF's Sentry?

6 Which mountain did Ian Thompson climb in a wheelchair?

7 Which supersonic airliner celebrated its 10th birthdy in 1986?

8 Whose album 'Double Fantasy' was a hit after his death?

9 Which US city became the home of the Rock and Roll Hall of Fame?

10 From which film did the song 'Take My Breath Away' come?

ANSWERS

1, ABBA 2, Hockey 3, Ian Botham 4, A giant panda 5, A converted 707 AWACS jet 6, Scafell Pike 7, Concorde (introduced to regular service in 1976) 8, John Lennon 9, Cleveland 10, Top Gun

QUIZ 270
QUESTIONS FROM THE EIGHTIES

1 Which Chancellor of the Exchequer resigned in 1989?

2 Who broke with his wife Robin Givens in 1988?

3 Who became Communist party boss in Moscow but was sacked in 1987?

4 As what was Sir A J Ayer noted: a) philosopher b) judge c) historian?

5 Which actor voiced Mr Magoo?

6 What game did Neil Foster play for England?

7 Which actress who died in 1989 was nominated 10 times for Oscars and won two?

8 Who became Hungary's ceremonial president in 1988, shortly before his death?

9 Which Filipino leader was shot dead in 1983 moments after leaving a plane?

10 Who played a prime minister in A Very British Coup (1988)?

ANSWERS

1, Nigel Lawson 2, Mike Tyson 3, Boris Yeltsin 4, a) 5, Jim Backus (who died in 1989) 6, Cricket 7, Bette Davis 8, Janos Kadar 9, Benigno Aquino 10, Ray McAnally

QUIZ 271
QUESTIONS FROM THE EIGHTIES

1 Who recorded the album 'True Blue'?

2 Who sang 'The Lady in Red' in 1986?

3 It was the artist's 24th release: what was unique about it?

4 Who sang 'Opportunities'?

5 And what was its sub-title?

6 Who wrote the song 'Papa Don't Preach'?

7 Which 1987 album was the first to enter both US and UK charts at No 1?

8 Which veteran surfers were back on the road in 1989?

9 Who sang 'Sealed with a Kiss'?

10 And who preceded him with a May '89 number one?

ANSWERS

1, Madonna 2, Chris De Burgh 3, It was his first UK Top 40 hit 4, Pet Shop Boys 5, '(Let's Make Lots of Money)' 6, Madonna 7, Whitney 8, The Beach Boys 9, Jason Donovan 10 Kylie Minogue

QUIZ 272
QUESTIONS FROM THE EIGHTIES

1 Which soccer team did the song 'Ossie's Dream' celebrate?

2 Who was Ossie?

3 Which country sent 'Susei' into space?

4 And who or what was it?

5 Who set a new mile record in July 1980?

6 What nationality was Alan Bond?

7 Where was the Victorian Football League?

8 Which championship was 100 years old in 1986?

9 What happened to Virgin Atlantic Challenger?

10 And what was it trying to do?

ANSWERS

1, Tottenham Hotspur 2, Osvaldo Ardiles 3, Japan 4, A spacecraft to investigate Halley's Comet 5, Steve Ovett 6, Australian 7. Australia 8, The world chess championship 9, It sank, in 1985 10, Set a new record for a trans-Atlantic water crossing

QUIZ 273

QUESTIONS FROM THE EIGHTIES

1   Which soccer team sang 'Here We Go'?

2   What was soccer star Butcher's first name?

3   Who rode Teenoso to win the Derby?

4   What year?

5   In what county was Kilverstone Wildlife Park?

6   Which country's capital was Port Moresby?

7   What was the Great Britain, being restored?

8   And who had designed it?

9   Which Asian country celebrated 10 years since reunification in 1985?

10   Who was Robert Graves?

ANSWERS

1, Everton 2, Terry 3, Lester Piggott 4, 1983 5, Norfolk 6, Papua New Guinea 7, A steamship 8, Isambard Kingdom Brunel 9, Vietnam 10, Poet and novelist (died 1985)

QUIZ 274
QUESTIONS FROM THE EIGHTIES

1 Which plane's secrets were revealed by a probe in 1986?

2 What prize did Wole Soyinka win that year?

3 Which potter's 200th anniversary was marked in 1983?

4 Of which hospital was Tadworth Court part?

5 And which group of patients did it treat?

6 Who was Ben de Haan?

7 And what did he sit on in April 1983?

8 Why was Black Rock Desert in the news?

9 Who revisited Treetops Lodge?

10 Where were 250 yew bows recovered from a soaking?

ANSWERS

1, Uranus 2, Nobel Prize for Literature 3, Josiah Spode 4, Great Ormond Street 5, Children 6, 1983 Grand National winning jockey 7, The horse Corbiere 8, A new land speed record was set there 9, The Queen and Duke of Edinburgh 10, On board the Tudor ship Mary Rose

QUIZ 275
QUESTIONS FROM THE NINETIES

1 Which musical instrument did Bill Clinton like to play?

2 What is the name of the Clintons' daughter?

3 What does DVD stand for?

4 What 90s phenomenon began in the 60s as ARPAnet?

5 Which Surrey player captained the England cricket team?

6 Which was John Prescot's favourite car?

7 Which British carmaker was unwanted by BMW as the 90s ended?

8 For which film did Gwyneth Paltrow win an Oscar?

9 Who wrote the original story The Witches, filmed in 1990?

10 Who starred as the Grand High Witch?

ANSWERS

1, Tenor saxophone 2, Chelsea 3, Digital Versatile (or Video) Disc 4, The Internet 5, Alec Stewart 6, Jaguar 7, Rover 8, Shakespeare In Love 9, Roald Dahl 10, Anjelica Houston

QUIZ 276
QUESTIONS FROM THE NINETIES

1 What was Norman Lamont's last job in government?

2 For whom did David Seaman play soccer?

3 Where was the Pergau Dam?

4 In which TV soap did Kevin and Sally split up?

5 Which veteran singer made the 'Duets' album?

6 Which novelist was a leading Tory crowd-rouser?

7 Who wrote the play Oleanna (1992)?

8 Kim Il Sung died in 1994: which country had he led ?

9 Who was Nadja Avermann?

10 A flower's 400th 'birthday 'was celebrated in the Netherlands in 1994. Which flower?

ANSWERS

1, Chancellor of the Exchequer 2, Arsenal 3, Malaysia 4, Coronation Street
5, Frank Sinatra 6, Jeffrey Archer 7, David Mamet 8, North Korea
9, A German 'super model' 10, The tulip

QUIZ 277

QUESTIONS FROM THE NINETIES

1 Who played Mr Bean on film and TV?

2 What nationality was the 1996 Nobel Prize-winner for Literature?

3 Where were the 1996 Olympic Games held?

4 Which ex-boxing champion lit the Olympic Flame?

5 Who became Canada's first woman prime minister?

6 Who declared that 'prison works'?

7 Was there really a 90s rap group called Insane Clown Posse?

8 In which country did the LDP lose power after 38 years?

9 What were the Royal Navy's new Vanguards?

10 Who was the number one ranking men's tennis player in 1990?

ANSWERS

1, Rowan Atkinson 2, Polish (Wislawa Szymborska) 3, Atlanta, Georgia
4, Mohammed Ali 5, Kim Campbell 6, UK Home Secretary Michael Howard
7, Yes 8, Japan 9, Submarines 10, Stefan Edberg

QUIZ 278

QUESTIONS FROM THE NINETIES

1 Who made a 1991 album called 'Waking Up the Neighbours'?

2 In which country did UNTAC operate?

3 For what activity was the Carlsberg Prize awarded?

4 Which US orchestra celebrated its 150th birthday in 1992?

5 Who played the US TV character Murphy Brown?

6 Why did Vice President Quayle criticize her character?

7 Is Pierre Boulez a musical conductor or a soccer coach?

8 Who won the woman's 100 metres at the '92 olympics?

9 And her country?

10 By what first name was Labour politician Dr Cunningham usually known?

ANSWERS

1, Bryan Adams 2, Cambodia 3, Architecture 4, New York Philharmonic 5, Candice Bergen 6, Murphy Brown had an illegitimate child 7, A musical conductor 8, Gail Devers 9, USA 10, Jack

QUIZ 279
QUESTIONS FROM THE NINETIES

1 What language was Gunter Grass writing in?

2 Where was P.V. Narasimha Rao prime minister?

3 Who headed a UK committee on standards of conduct in public life?

4 What was the estimated population of the UK in 1995: a)50 million b)55 million c)58 million?

5 Which new country's capital was Kiev?

6 Which party did Robert Dole represent?

7 Which general declined to run in that election?

8 Who wrote An Awfully Big Adventure?

9 In which country was the first Ibsen Stage Festival held?

10 Which yellow puppet starred in a 1999 TV ad?

ANSWERS

1, German 2, India 3, Lord Nolan 4, c) 5, Ukraine 6, Republican 7, Colin Powell 8, Beryl Bainbridge 9, Norway 10, Flat Eric

QUIZ 280
QUESTIONS FROM THE NINETIES

1 Where was the Getty Center being built: a)Paris b)Los Angeles c) Moscow?

2 Which London borough was chosen as the site for the Millennium Dome?

3 Where was the Tsing Ma bridge built?

4 In which city did an art exhibition of Charles Rennie Mackintosh's work open in 1996?

5 Which nuclear power station was 40 years old in 1996?

6 In what art-form had Rafael Kubelik been distinguished?

7 In which city did a disco fire kill 159 people (1996)?

8 What meteorological phenomenon upset the 1995 skiing season?

9 What country did Moses Kiptanui run for?

10 Who wrote a poem to the Queen Mother on her 95th birthday?

ANSWERS

1, Los Angeles 2, Greenwich 3, Hong Kong 4, Glasgow 5, Calder Hall (UK)
6, Music, as conductor and composer 7, Manila, in the Philippines
8, Warm weather, no snow 9, Kenya 10, Ted Hughes

QUIZ 281
QUESTIONS FROM THE NINETIES

1   Of which magazine was Tina Brown made editor in chief in 1992?

2   Which schoolboy wizard topped the best-selling lists ?

3   Who wrote Diana: Her True Story?

4   Which star published a collection of erotic pictures in 1992?

5   The book title?

6   Which explorer's Quincentenary was marked in 1992?

7   What date is officially his day in the USA?

8   Which British soccer team beat Parma to win the 1994 European Cup-Winner's Cup?

9   Which country did Will Carling captain?

10 And in which sport?

ANSWERS

1, The New Yorker 2, Harry Potter 3, Andrew Morton 4, Madonna 5, Sex
6, Columbus 7, October 12 8, Arsenal 9, England 10, Rugby Union

QUIZ 282

QUESTIONS FROM THE NINETIES

1 Which doll was 35 years old in 1994?

2 Which rival doll was the subject of a 1991 'copycat' lawsuit?

3 Which Muslim country banned the doll?

4 Who resigned as director of Kenya Wildlife Service in 1994?

5 What accident had befallen him the year before?

6 What was Reba McEntire's musical style?

7 Where was an unusual shadow-clock installed in a railway station ceiling?

8 Who stood down as Labour's deputy leader after the '92 general election?

9 Which country's cattle herd seemed to be growing the fastest in the mid '90s?

10 What was Australopithecus afarensis, whose bones were being found in Africa?

ANSWERS

1, Barbie 2, Miss America 3, Kuwait 4, Richard Leakey 5, A plane crash in which he lost both legs 6, Country and Western 7, New York 8, Roy Hattersley 9, China's 10, An early hominid ('ape-man')

QUIZ 283

QUESTIONS FROM THE NINETIES

1 Whose nickname was 'Slick Willy'?

2 Which Royal had a hip replacement in 1998?

3 Where was Carla Tucker executed?

4 Who was chairman of microsoft?

5 What was QVC?

6 What post did Lord Irvine hold in the UK?

7 In which TV show did Pamela Anderson make her name?

8 With which band did her husband perform?

9 And his name?

10 Who led Ulster's Unionists as the decade ended ?

ANSWERS

1, President Clinton 2, The Queen Mother 3, Texas, USA 4, Bill Gates
5, A US shopping channel 6, Lord Chancellor 7, Baywatch 8, Motley Crue
9, Tommy Lee 10, David Trimble

QUIZ 284
QUESTIONS FROM THE NINETIES

1   A 90s 'celebrity'-: Denise --- ----- . Who?

2   Who lost his job as England soccer coach in 1999?

3   Who or what was Dana International?

4   Who decided to run for London mayor and get back the top job in the city after 14 years?

5   Which newspaper portrayed the Tory leader as a parrot upside-down?

6   Who was the Tory leader?

7   Who was Theodore Kaczynski, jailed in the USA?

8   Which Labour minister was 'outed' in 1998?

9   Who had iced water thrown at him at the Brit Awards?

10 To whom did James Major become engaged, and marry?

ANSWERS

1, Van Outen 2, Glen Hoddle 3, The Israeli winner of the 1998 Eurovision Song contest 4, Ken Livingstone 5, The Sun 6, William Hague 7, The so-called 'Una Bomber' 8, Peter Mandelson 9, John Prescott 10, Emma Noble

QUIZ 285
QUESTIONS FROM THE NINETIES

1 Which Rolling Stone had a marital tiff in 1998?

2 What coveted trophy did Jana Novotna finally win?

3 Who marched at Drumcree?

4 From whom did Bruce Willis say he was parting (1998)?

5 Who held his 50th birthday bash at Highgrove in 1998?

6 For whom had David Shayler once worked?

7 Which animals on the run became celebrities in Wiltshire?

8 Which new pill gave a lift to men in 1998?

9 Which murderer was cleared 45 years after he was hanged?

10 Who went back into space 26 years on?

ANSWERS

1, Mick Jagger 2, The Wimbledon ladies singles 3, Northern Ireland Orangemen 4, Demi Moore 5, Prince Charles 6, MI-5 7, Two Tamworth pigs 8, Viagra 9, Derek Bentley 10, John Glenn

QUIZ 286

QUESTIONS FROM THE NINETIES

1 Which club finally allowed women in?

2 From which film did the song 'You Can Keep Your Hat On' come?

3 Which lady from The Cruise became a singing star?

4 In which TV series did Calista Flockhart make her name?

5 Which actress appeared in The Blue Room?

6 Which ex-soccer player appeared in Lock, Stock And Two Smoking Barrels?

7 Which Chilean general came to London and stayed a while?

8 Which government minister did 'something foolish' on Clapham Common'?

9 From which post did he resign?

10 For what was Marco Pierre White famous?

ANSWERS

1, The MCC 2, The Full Monty 3, Jane McDonald 4, Ally McBeal 5, Nicole Kidman 6, Vinnie Jones 7, General Pinochet 8, Ron Davies 9, Welsh Secretary 10, Cooking

QUIZ 287
QUESTIONS FROM THE NINETIES

1 Who said in 1998 'the time to stop the killing is now, before it spreads'?

2 Of which troublespot was he/she speaking?

3 Which country told tourists not to kiss publicly?

4 Which princess suffered a stroke on Mustique?

5 Whom did Manchester United beat to win the European Champions Cup in 1999?

6 Of which country was Jigme Singye Wangchuk king?

7 Who said he thought stability was a 'sexy thing'?

8 Who ate cabbage pie on his 67th birthday?

9 Who said he was 'pissed off trying to make this thing work'?

10 Where was TV banned by the new government?

ANSWERS

1, Madeline Albright 2, Kosovo 3, India 4, Princess Margaret 5, Bayern Munich 6, Bhutan 7, Tony Blair 8, Boris Yeltsin 9, Gerry Adams (of the N. Ireland peace talks) 10, Afghanistan

QUIZ 288
QUESTIONS FROM THE NINETIES

1 Which national leader announced his retirement on New Year's Eve 1999?

2 Which UK politician said goodbye to Health to campaign in London?

3 Which veteran football manager went home to rescue the Magpies?

4 What prize did José Saramayo win?

5 Which river was to have a new pedestrian-only bridge for the Millennium?

6 Who became Labour's new Home Secretary in 1997?

7 Who became the highest-paid woman on British TV?

8 On which show had her maths wizardry made her a celebrity?

9 Who wrote a book called Charles: Victim or Villain?

10 From which TV show was Richard Bacon sacked?

ANSWERS

1, Boris Yeltsin 2, Frank Dobson 3, Bobby Robson 4, Nobel Prize for Literature 5, The Thames in London 6, Jack Straw 7, Carol Vorderman 8, Countdown 9, Penny Junor 10, Blue Peter

QUIZ 289
QUESTIONS FROM THE NINETIES

1 What did Louise Greenfarb have 17,000 examples of in 1996?

2 Which actor, who died in 1999, played General Patton on screen?

3 Which city changed its name to Kolkata in July 1999?

4 Which country's population topped the 1 billion mark in 1999?

5 What was cooked in Rotherham in August 1991 to celebrate Yorkshire Day?

6 What super-tall structure fell down in Poland in 1991?

7 Which British actress appeared on TV in 1991 aged 100?

8 Complete the 1993 movie title: The Long Kiss------?

9 Which 11-year-old starred in My Girl (1991)?

10 Which world title did Larry Kahn of the USA win for the 14th time in 1995?

ANSWERS

1, Fridge magnets 2, George C. Scott 3, Calcutta 4, India's 5, A giant Yorkshire Pudding 6, The Warsaw Radio mast 7, Gwen Ffrancon-Davies 8, Goodnight 9, Macaulay Culkin 10, Tiddlywinks

QUIZ 290
QUESTIONS FROM THE NINETIES

1 Complete the TV title: Murder, She -----?

2 Who starred in Prime Suspect 3?

3 Which country launched the Geotail satellite?

4 What nationality was GP driver Roland Ratzenberger?

5 At which race track was he killed in 1994?

6 What do the initials GATT stand for?

7 In which business did Abode and Aldus merge: a) software
b) fashion c) housebuilding?

8 Which plant-crop was hit by disease in India and China in the mid-90s: a) rice b) silk c) cotton?

9 Which sea saw the worst-ever ferry disaster (1994)?

10 Which country's art featured in a US exhibition called 'Treasures from Heaven'?

ANSWERS

1, Wrote 2, Helen Mirren 3, Japan 4, Austrian 5, San Marino 6, General Agreement on Tariffs and Trade 7, a) 8, c) 9, Baltic 10, Armenia

QUIZ 291

QUESTIONS FROM THE NINETIES

1 Which city featured in the film The Commitments?

2 Which country is reckoned to have the biggest Kurdish population in 1991: a) Iraq b) Turkey c) USSR?

3 Which country had the biggest fleet of merchant ships in 1990?

4 Which sport staged its sixth world championship at Perth, Australia in 1991?

5 Which South African won the 1991 Nobel Prize for Literature?

6 Of which country was Sultan Azian Shah ruler?

7 Which British royal made her first visit to Pakistan in 1991?

8 In which country was the BJP active?

9 Was the British Army's Challenger a tank, a gun, or a missile?

10 Which western lakes were invaded by mussels from Asia?

ANSWERS

1, Dublin 2, b) 3, Liberia 4, Swimming 5, Nadine Gordimer 6, Malaysia
7, Princess Diana 8, India 9, A tank 10, The Great Lakes

QUIZ 292
QUESTIONS FROM THE NINETIES

1 Which European nation dominated international basketball in 1990?

2 Who beat Mike Tyson in ten rounds?

3 Which country was also known as Myanmar?

4 What aircraft was the star of the film Memphis Belle?

5 Which London gangsters' career was chronicled on film?

6 Who was chairman of the US Joint Chiefs of Staff?

7 In which continent was the black-faced lion tamarin discovered?

8 And what kind of creature was it?

9 Was Rifat Ozbeck a fashion designer or politician?

10 Which Yorkshire city had a new stadium for the 1991 World Student Games?

ANSWERS

1, Yugoslavia 2, James 'Buster' Douglas 3, Burma 4, A WW2 B-17 bomber
5, The Krays 6, General Colin Powell 7, South America 8, A monkey
9, A fashion designer 10, Sheffield

QUIZ 293
QUESTIONS FROM THE NINETIES

1 Which judge retired, saying the work was too strenuous?.

2 Which country held its first-ever free election?

3 Which Nobel prize did Jerome Friedman share?

4 Which British golfer won the US Masters?

5 Who challenged Margaret Thatcher for the Tory leadership?

6 Who was the new editor of The Times (March 1990)?

7 Who was Alice Munro?

8 Who said 'I do write too many books'?

9 And which detective featured in many of them?

10 For whom did Matthew Maynard play cricket?

ANSWERS

1, US Justice William J Brennan 2, Mongolia 3, Physics 4, Nick Faldo
5, Michael Heseltine 6, Simon Jenkins 7, A Canadian novelist 8, Ruth
Rendell 9, DCI Reg Wexford 10, Glamorgan and England

QUIZ 294
QUESTIONS FROM THE NINETIES

1   By what name was the community charge better known?

2   In which country was Jean Chretien a politician?

3   In which city did the Almeida Theatre attract praise?

4   Which writer's Narnia books were a hit on TV and stage?

5   In which country was Benazir Bhutto deposed in 1990?

6   What game did the Seibu Lions play?

7   Was Grete Waitz a runner, a singer, or a TV cook?

8   Which country became the Commonwealth's 50th member in 1990?

9   What did the initials PCC mean in the media world from 1991?

10 Who wrote a long poem called Omeros?

ANSWERS

1, The poll tax 2, Canada 3, London 4, C.S. Lewis 5, Pakistan 6, Baseball (in Japan) 7, A Norwegian runner 8, Namibia 9, Press Complaints Commission 10, Derek Walcott

QUIZ 295
QUESTIONS FROM THE NINETIES

1 Who was Robson Green's singing partner in 1995?

2 Which artists had had a 1990 hit with the same song?

3 And which veteran 1990s broadcaster topped the charts with it in 1955?

4 Which country had the most radio stations in the mid-90s?

5 Did it have a) 5 million b) 7 million c) 12 million?

6 Which group released the album Stars in 1991?

7 Which country won the 1992 Eurovision Song Contest with Why Me?

8 And the singer?

9 Which highest-ever buildings were designed by Cesar Peli?

10 In which continent were they?

ANSWERS

1, Jerome Flynn 2, The Righteous Brothers (Unchained Melody) 3, Jimmy Young 4, USA 5, c) 6, Simply Red 7, Ireland 8, Linda Martin 9, The Petronas Towers 10, Asia (Malaysia)

QUIZ 296
QUESTIONS FROM THE NINETIES

1 Which campaign won the 1997 Nobel Peace Prize?

2 Where was the Teatro Real reopened?

3 And what is it?

4 The biggest Commonwealth country (by population) celebrated 50 years of independence in 1997. What is it?

5 At which massacre site there did the Queen lay a wreath?

6 What game did Florida Marlins play?

7 Who became Irish president in 1997?

8 From which country did the soccer club Dynamo Minsk come?

9 Of what organisation was Emeka Anyaoku head?

10 Which city was said to be the most seriously polluted: a) New York b) Moscow c) Mexico City?

ANSWERS

1, International Campaign to Ban Landmines 2, Madrid 3, An opera house
4, India 5, Amritsar 6, Baseball 7, Mary McAleese 8, Belarus
9, Commonwealth Secretariat 10, c)

QUIZ 297

QUESTIONS FROM THE NINETIES

1 Which England footballer appeared for a French team in the 1991 European Cup Final?

2 Which team did he represent?

3 Which actress starred in the 1990 film Not Without My Daughter?

4 What sport did John Whitaker compete in?

5 Which famous Manchester speedway track faced an uncertain future?

6 Who became the youngest-ever Welsh soccer international in 1991?

7 Which was the world's largest retailer in the 90s?

8 In which city did the UK's largest strike end in 1994?

9 Any idea when it had begun?

10 Which country had the biggest national debt in the decade?

ANSWERS

1, Chris Waddle 2, Marseille 3, Sally Field 4, Show jumping 5, Belle Vue
6, Ryan Giggs 7, Wal-Mart Stores, Inc 8, Sheffield 9, 1986 10, The USA

QUIZ 298
QUESTIONS FROM THE NINETIES

1 Which Tom starred in Mission: Impossible?

2 Who was his off-screen wife?

3 Was Alek Wek a) a model b) a scientist or c) a TV presenter?

4 In which country did Maurice Papon go on trial?

5 With what was he charged?

6 Which new library was hastily fitted with shutters to keep the sun off its books?

7 In which country was the Robben Island Museum?

8 Who was its most famous former inmate?

9 Which animal was declared the only ancestor of the domestic dog?

10 Who wrote the novel Quarantine?

ANSWERS

1, Tom Cruise 2, Nicole Kidman 3, a) 4, France 5, War crimes in World War II 6, France's National Library 7, South Africa 8, Nelson Mandela 9, The wolf 10, Jim Crace